Anything Beats Milking Cows

W. Peyton George

D1736281

Table of Contents

Acknowledgments – 4

1. Introduction – 9

2. My Lineage and the Early Years – 10

3. The Roughneck Days – 19

4. Oklahoma City Police Department – 29

5. J. Edgar Hoover's FBI – 46

6. USDA, Advance Man, and the Army – 92

7. Practicing Law – 122

8. Family – 163

9. Tales, Trips, and Characters – 189

10. Conclusion – 226

Appendix – 228

Acknowledgments

I have had many people throughout my lifetime who helped me along the way. They sometimes picked me up, dusted me off, and provided guidance that motivated me to keep trying. Many are no longer living, so I can only do my best to pay it forward for them. Once I start naming, I am sure I will miss many.

I can start with my dad, William Peyton George, aka Dub George or W. P. George. He instilled a work ethic in me.

My grandfather, Thomas Houston George, was a key role model, businessman and rancher.

My grandmothers, Florence Caroline Orr George, and Lenora Carter Kite. Both were sources of support and encouragement. My Grandmother George had many sayings, probably not original with her. Some of her bests were, "A little discretion saves a lot of discussion", "If a task is once begun, never finish until it's done", and "He or she is best educated who has touched life in most places."

My uncles Clyde Wyant, Houston George, Sam Kite, Haskell Kite, Frank Kite, and T. G. (Coot) Simpson. They were available for guidance and career information.

General Richard H. Thompson was my company commander for basic training at Fort Chaffee. Arkansas, in 1957. I was then a private E-1, and he was a captain. He had walked into Germany in World War II as a sergeant with an infantry division and stayed in the Army afterwards. I would cross paths to work with him again when he was a four-star general and I was a colonel. I was proud to have been a "Thompson's Tiger." When I placed my wife Nancy's ashes in Arlington National Cemetery on a cold snowy day in February 2003, he and his wife Pat were there. He saw me as a kid off the farm he had motivated and was pleased that I had turned out okay.

John R. Robertson, an oil-and-gas lawyer and commander of the 95th MP Company, my Army Reserve Unit, got me a direct commission in the Military Police Corps. We later worked together on legal matters.

General Robert Kingston, Commander Rapid Joint Task Force (RDJTF) which evolved into Central Command (CENTCOM) whom I serve as his legal advisor for military exercises over all the branches of service. Heady stuff for an Army Reserve JAG officer/ DC Street lawyer.

Major General Wayne P. Jackson, Chief Probation Officer U. S Courts. He a former Tulsa Police Officer and I a former Oklahoma City Police officer. I served as his SJA (Military equivalent of General Counsel) at the 352nd Civil Affairs Command, Riverdale, MD and again at the 97th ARCOM, Fort Meade, MD. The 97th had fourteen thousand Army reservists scattered from Maine to Florida, literally most types of military units, and more aircraft than most airlines.

Those several drillers or crew chiefs on oil field rotary drilling rigs who taught me how to be a competent derrickman and roughneck and to enjoy the work when I needed jobs the most: Buster Dickerson, Bruce Russell, Tom Biggs, Herbie Bird, Ivan Salters, Loren Groom, J. T. McConnell, Johnnie Nickerson, Arley Neeley, Chester Nichols, and several others I no longer recall.

Hobson H. Adcock, who served as my life coach

during my stint at the FBI.

Cartha (Deke) DeLoach, assistant director FBI, who later became a Vice President of PepsiCo for government relations. I worked for him at both places.

Hershel Caver, my supervisor in the Richmond, Virginia, FBI office, who re-drafted the reports I sent in from Lynchburg on Dictaphone Belts to make me look good. He told me to join my Oklahoma State Society if I ever served in Washington, D.C. for the contacts I made there. It was great advice.

Secretary of Agriculture Dr. Earl Butz, the absolute best boss I ever had. I served on his Congressional Liaison Staff and as one of his Advance men during the 1972 Presidential Campaign.

Jim Nelson, friend, neighbor, and mentor who found us our first house and collaborated with me on spy stuff during the cold war.

Forrest Putman, friend, and FBI special agent in charge (SAC). He introduced me to the right FBI officials and provided great advice.

John Meade, a tough New Yorker, and my partner at the Atlantic City FBI office. He made sure we got the job done despite a jerk of a senior resident agent who did not want me to be there.

E. Joseph Hillings, my friend and neighbor who headed the Washington, DC offices of several large U.S. multinational companies. He exposed me to corporate lobbying with Congress and got me on some great trips.

Stephen B. King, my friend and fellow former FBI agent. He took the job as bodyguard for Martha Mitchell, colorful wife of former Attorney John Mitchell, during the Watergate era when I turned it down. Steve went on to be a businessman and political powerhouse in Wisconsin. He ran the 2016 Republican Convention in Cleveland where I and my companion had complete access, and later served as U.S. Ambassador to the Czech Republic.

Marshall Burkes, my friend and fellow "okie" whom I served with at the Farmers Home Administration. Marshall, a PhD Agriculture Economist, and I, a lawyer and former FBI Agent, were hired by former Congressman James V. Smith, the administrator, we suppose as potential "yes men" to help get him re-elected to Congress if we spent much of the agencies' budget in Oklahoma. Marshall put together a cutting-edge block sale of agency promissory notes with the top wall Street underwriters which kept the agency financially sound in challenging times and I got to meet most of them at that time.

Dr. Thomas Cowden, Assistant Secretary, and former Dean at Michigan State. He later plucked me out of that FmHA mess and put me on the personal staff of Secretary of Agriculture Clifford Hardin who was succeeded by Earl Butz.

Lieutenant "Ace" Williams, my shift lieutenant with the Oklahoma City Police Department. He often told us kids, "Shake a hand when you can, make a friend when you can." He taught me how to be a good police officer.

Larry Cates, who introduced me to many key people when I came to Washington, D.C.

Robert Cavanaugh and Lee Charlton, my two best friends, going all the way back to my police and FBI days.

Stanley McKiernan, Los Angeles Attorney whom I worked with and referred me great cases.

Don Jacubec, friend and banker.

Ken Baumann at bookinsix.com, for helping me get

this book edited, designed, and published.

Ed Palm who helped me get this organized. I could not have done without him.

And last, but not least, Benjamin Weiner, who gave me lots of career advice on both business deals and picking the right law firms.

Introduction

These are the stories of one of the luckiest guys in the world, one who has lived the Great American Dream. Growing up on a dairy farm, my younger brother Tom and I helped our dad milk as many as thirty-five cows every morning before school and every evening after school, seven days a week, 365 days a year. That was a great motivator to do something else. Life's challenges were easily handled from then on: Oil field roughneck and derrickman in five states; Oklahoma City police officer; Military Police officer; Judge Advocate Generals Corps (JAG) officer; FBI Special Agent, with service in Richmond and Lynchburg, Virginia, Newark and Atlantic City, New Jersey, and in the Washington D.C. field office (it was there that I ran spy cases). Moving from the FBI I served as a Congressional liaison officer for two Secretaries of Agriculture, Clifford Hardin, and Earl Butz, and as a political advance man in a Nixon – Ford presidential campaign. Upon leaving the government, I became a partner in two consecutive large law firms. During it all, I rose from private to colonel in the Army Reserve, serving for a total of thirty-four years.

It has been a great ride.

My Lineage and the Early Years

My great-great grandfather, Russell George, according to the 1860 Alabama census, was born about 1833 in South Carolina. He first appears on the record of Benton County (now Calhoun County), Alabama, in the mid-1850s. He obtained eighty acres of land at a time when most people were only getting forty acres. According to documents that he signed for his land, he could read and write. He signed sworn statements for his brother-in-law, Alberter M. C. Pettit, to obtain his federal land, and vice versa. Other than that, he left few tracks, and most of the courthouse records were burned by Union forces during the Civil War.

As far as I can tell from tracing George family genealogy, we descend from a barmaid in a tavern on the Linder Plantation in Spartanburg County, South Carolina. Her name was Jenny George. She had several children who apparently took her last name. There are several sources indicating that a Hezekiah George may have been the father, but if so, he left no tracks. I hope my DNA genealogy efforts will someday clarify this situation.

Some years ago, I received a message from a person who was helping her niece get into the Daughters of the American Revolution (DAR). She reported that her ancestor Jefferson Nathaniel George, in Spartanburg, South Carolina, had two brothers. One, Jeremiah or Jerry, went to Brevard, North Carolina. That I have confirmed about Jeremiah. The other brother, Russell, went to Alabama. I assume Russell to be my great-great grandfather.

I have a 111 marker DNA match with Alex George, a descendant of Jeremiah. I assume all three were brothers. Jeremiah and Russell had the same father according to DNA. Jefferson Nathaniel George does not match them on the descendant DNA male tests. They probably had the same mother, as they look alike in photographs. All served in the Civil War, but only Jeremiah survived.

Russell was in Company F of the 9th Battalion, which later became Company F of the 58th Alabama. He was in the Battle of Chickamauga and died of pneumonia shortly after the battle. He was probably at the Battle of Shiloh earlier.

His nine-year-old son, my great grandfather Thomas Jefferson George, reported that his father came home sick after the Battle of Chickamauga, went back, and never came home again. They lived over the state line in Alabama. The only Civil War record I have, other than some muster rolls, is that he had a ten-dollar gold piece when he died. A surgeon received it. Six months later, there is a record of the surgeon giving the gold piece to the widow. They seem to have kept better property records than records on people back then. He was probably buried along the railroad tracks somewhere in Georgia near the Chickamauga Battlefield.

Our George family migrated to Denton County, Texas, and then descendants scattered all over the world. My great grandfather Thomas Jefferson George was Russell George's only son. He had four sisters. Thomas originally came to Texas to live with Arelius Coffey in Denton County. Later, his mother and two of his sisters followed him. My grandfather, Thomas Houston George, was born in Aubrey (Denton County), Texas, and grew up there. He and a classmate, C. M. Mays, came to Oklahoma, and started a string of lumber yards in small towns. It was known as the C. M. Mays Lumber Company. My grandmother, Florence Caroline Orr George, was from Denton, Texas. Her father was Peyton Randolph Orr, and her brothers had the bank in Denton.

My father was William Peyton George Sr., and my mother was Jodie Lee Kite George. I was born in Valley View Hospital in Ada, Oklahoma. My parents had a 210-acre farm located near Ada, Oklahoma, on Sandy Creek.

Electricity Brought Running Water

I was about five or six years old when we got electricity on the farm. I recall sticking a bobby pin in the electrical outlet. I never did that again. Reminds me of a favorite quote attributed to General Omar Bradley: "Good judgment comes from experience and experience comes from bad judgment." I have had lots of experience.

Electricity brought running water and indoor toilets and put an end to kerosene lamps. Before then we had an outhouse, and we got all our drinking water from a water well and from a cistern that caught water off the roof of the house. A pitcher pump was beside the kitchen sink. It pumped water from the cistern. Before we had electricity, we also drew buckets of water from the well. As kids, we took baths in #10 washtubs, and my mother cooked on a wood stove. We had a fireplace, and we later used butane heaters to heat the house.

When I was a small child, my father was gone occasionally as a trucker. He hauled lumber from southeastern Oklahoma or from Colorado to my grandfather's lumber yard located in Ada, Oklahoma. This was before tornado warnings. It seemed that every time it got cloudy, my mother would take me and my younger brothers Tom and Lee to safety in the storm cellar where the glass fruit jars of canned goods were stored.

My dad eventually ended up with dairy cows, and we ran a Grade A dairy. He, my brother Tom, and I milked as many as seventeen cows by hand and as many as thirty-five after we obtained electric milking machines. Milking all those cows every morning before school, and every evening after school, was a great motivator to do something else. It was a 24/7 job. We raised hogs and showed dairy cattle and hogs at the local county fair. We grew alfalfa and corn.

My boyhood friends included Robert Skaggs, Cork-ie Hudson, Charles Maxey, Charles Dyer, Alvin Gilley, George Hill, Wayne Tiner, Milton (Cub) Biggs and his brother Wayne Biggs. We attended school together, hunted and fished, and did farm work together early on. Later, some of us worked together in the oil fields. Boy-hood friend Charles Dyer and I also worked together as officers with the Oklahoma City Police Department.

I belonged to the 4-H Club in grade school. When I was about 14 years old, I had the First Place Holstein dairy cow at the county fair. The prize was an expens-es-paid trip to the National Dairy Congress at Water-loo, Iowa. In high school, I had four years of agriculture courses and belonged to the Future Farmers of America (FFA).

Our elementary and high school classes were held in the same small square three-story brick building. There were four classrooms per floor with two grades per class-room. Sometimes we rode the bus to school, sometimes we would walk, and sometimes I even rode a horse. We boys were pulled out of school on occasion to fight range fires. We might have a pickup with a 55-gallon drum of water. We would dip gunny sacks in the water then swat out the grass fires.

When I was about fifteen, I was a page boy for state representative George R. Collins at the Oklahoma State Capitol. That experience caused me to consider the possibility of a public office later in life.

Class Trips

There were only twenty-six of us in my senior class. Our rural high school had so few students that instead of a senior trip, we had a junior-senior trip and went every other year. That way, we would have enough students to fill a bus. In 1953 I was a junior. We had spent a year raising money with pie suppers, donkey ball games, and the like to fund a class trip. Someone had decided we should go to Washington, D.C. We junior and senior Latta High School students boarded an old Denco Bus Line bus with our luggage piled up on top toward the back of the bus. This was before the interstate highway system, and it was a long ride.

I recall our going through the weight stations in Indiana and Ohio. At each, we boys had to get on our hands and knees and crawl up to the front of the bus. We could then get some more weight on the front axle and off the overloaded rear axle while not being seen by the officials who ran the scales. In Washington, D.C. we stayed at tourist homes near Dupont Circle.

One evening, several of us juniors, wearing our Latta Oklahoma Future Farmer of America (FFA) jackets, wandered into the Mayflower hotel. Off the block-long lobby, there was a lounge or night club with an orchestra and a female singer. We congregated in the hallway out front, and I struck up a conversation with the maître-d' Being from a dry state, we had never seen a place where liquor was sold and served. The maître-d' proceeded to tell us he was friends with Roy J Turner, then the Governor of Oklahoma. This was obviously the governor's watering hole when in D.C. He told us Governor Turner had once shown him a $33 million government check that he had just picked up in Washington, D.C., to build the Turner Turnpike from Tulsa to Oklahoma City.

Being the spokesperson for our group, I asked how we could get inside. He told us that if we would get coats and ties on, he would seat us in a corner and serve us soft drinks. We ran back to our quarters near Dupont Circle, donned our sport coats and ties, and ran back down Connecticut Avenue to the Mayflower Hotel. Our new best friend, the Maître-d', who knew our Governor, seated us inside the lounge with the live entertainment. This is one of the high points of our junior-senior trip for me, along with taking the trolley to Glen Echo Amusement Park, touring the Capitol, seeing the monuments, and visiting Arlington National Cemetery.

I made straight A's for twelve years in school and never took a book home. This was an indication of what a poor education we had in comparison to the rest of the world. I would learn that the hard way when I started at the University of Oklahoma for my first semester in the fall of 1954. I wanted to be a petroleum engineer but spent the first semester at Oklahoma University with remedial courses. I transferred to East Central in Ada, Oklahoma, my hometown, where I picked up enough math courses to survive later. After a stint in the Army,

I returned to Oklahoma University, this time as a mechanical engineering student. Petroleum engineer jobs were scarce, as the oil industry was then in a downturn. I supported myself by working on drilling rigs at night. I later joined the Oklahoma City Police Department at the suggestion of my friend Charles Dyer.

After getting on to the Oklahoma City Police Department, I completed a summer session at Oklahoma City University and then commuted back to Oklahoma University (OU) with fellow officers Bob Macy and Ray LeGrande. Both were in law school. After another semester at OU, tired of working all night and attending class all day, as well as driving back and forth to Norman, I switched to Central State, now University of Central Oklahoma (UCO) in Edmond, which was closer and less of a commute than Norman. I had already acquired almost enough math and physics for a degree there and wanted out of college. I was honored later as a Distinguished Former Student at UCO. As soon as I graduated in 1961 from UCO, I began at Oklahoma City University Law School at night while still a police officer.

The Problem with Names

Dale Carnegie always said, "A person's name is the sweetest sound in any language." My father was named William Peyton George, and I was named William Peyton George Junior. However, he was never called by those names. His Okie nickname was Dub. So, I was Little Dub or Dub Junior. My mother, until she died, still called me Dub Junior. In the Army, I was Private George or Lieutenant George, and on the Oklahoma City Police Department I was Officer W.P. George. When I went to the FBI Academy, I was instructed to use my payroll signature of first name, middle initial, and last name. My credentials thus were William P. George Jr. all during my first office assignment at Richmond and as resident agent in Lynchburg, Virginia. Everybody wanted to be chummy and called me Bill.

One never gets used to it. For example, if you have been Mary all your life and now everybody wants to call you Susie, it grates on you. So, when I got to New Jersey, I went back to just W. P. George, informally.

I was in a bar one night with a friend, Kenny Moyer, my drinking buddy, and fellow Masonic Lodge Member. I was complaining about names per the above. I then had orders for a transfer to Washington, D.C. Kenny and I sketched out names on a napkin and finally produced "W. Peyton George." Upon arrival at my new assignment at the Washington Field office, I went down the street to FBI headquarters and had my credentials changed to W. Peyton George. It has worked out great ever since because it is a good professional name. I had a great grandfather named Peyton Randolph Orr.

Unfortunately, with the requirements of the TSA, everyone is being moved back to the first name, middle initial, and last name for frequent flyer and other I.D. cards. I have encountered that problem again, with people wanting to call me Bill. I almost caused a similar problem for my son. When he was born, we named him Shelley Peyton George. Shelley was a prominent poet my wife liked. After we got out of the hospital, and took him around with us, folks would ask, "What's the baby's name?" We would say, "Shelley Peyton George." Then they would say, "Oh, it's a little girl." So, I rushed down to the D.C. vital records agency and changed the birth certificate to Richard Peyton George. It no doubt saved him from a lot of grief.

The Roughneck Days

Upon graduating from Latta High School near Ada, Oklahoma, I worked off and on in the oil fields in Oklahoma, Kansas, Utah, Texas, and Louisiana from age seventeen to twenty-two. This was a popular thing to do at the time with good pay at $1.50 to $1.70 per hour. I worked on many diverse types of drilling rigs, even a steam rig once, and for many different drilling companies and drillers. A driller is the crew chief for the shift. The shift normally consisted of two roughnecks, or floor hands, and one derrickman, plus the driller.

In one year alone I had 12 W-2 tax forms. Some jobs might last a few days, while others might last as long as a month. From 1954 to 1959, I attended college full-time, sometimes driving 50 to 80 miles to and from the night shifts on some drilling rig to make day classes.

I started in late May 1954 as a crew member or roughneck on my first oil field job with the G.R. Mason Drilling Company. It was owned by G. R. (Chock) Mason whose children attended Latta High School where I had just graduated. I worked on this rig called a double. It pulled the two 30-foot joints of drill pipe at one time when bringing all the drill pipe out of the hole to change a drill bit. Mason had built the rig in Arizona and used it to drill water wells before moving back to Pontotoc County, Oklahoma, to become a contract driller for oil. I worked two weeks there as a roughneck or floor hand until we finished that well—at which point the rig was "stacked" or put out of service.

One of The Worst Days of My Life

I decided next to seek my fortune around Liberal, Kansas, where there was an oil boom at the time. I drove to Liberal in my 1951 Studebaker. I got a job briefly in the machine shop of Midwestern Drillers.

One might say that I started at the top in the oil fields. After working in that machine shop for a few days, I really wanted to get back on rotary drilling rigs. I called a driller named Buster Dickerson of Guymon, Oklahoma, as he had posted the need for a derrickman on the chalk board at the Blue Goose Café in Liberal. This was the way job openings were posted for oil field workers back then. He had the evening shift on a rig operating eleven miles north of Buffalo, Oklahoma, just below the Kansas line. I spoke with him over the phone, and in hindsight, there was obviously a huge breakdown of communication. I was a seventeen-year-old kid, six feet tall, and weighed one hundred twenty pounds. I had little experience in the oil field. He needed a derrickman and thought I was experienced. I had thought I had merely indicated that I was "willing to be a derrickman." The next afternoon I met up with the rest of the crew members in Buffalo, Oklahoma.

Our crew consisted of the driller or crew chief, Buster Dickerson, his 15-year-old son and a 19-year-old on his first well, and me with two weeks experience in the oil patch. From Buffalo, Oklahoma, we drove north to the drilling rig located just south of the Kansas border to begin our 3PM to 11PM shift (known as evening tour, pronounced "tower"). We came over a hill in view of what was to me the biggest drilling rig in the world—a

Lee C. Moore triple derrick. Not only that, but the day shift we were to relieve had just finished pulling all three thousand feet of drill pipe out of the hole to replace the drill bit. The only rig I had worked on before had a maximum depth of about 1,500 feet, while this enormous rig could drill several miles deep. This entire string of drill pipe was racked into three joints of 30- or 33-foot pipe, six inches in diameter, screwed together and packed into rows. Furthermore, they were running twenty-seven drill collars. Drill collars are very heavy drill pipes that are run just on top of the drill bit to provide weight and help keep the hole straight.

The position I had signed up for, Derrickman, works on a platform attached to the derrick or mast typically eighty-five feet or more above the rig floor. The derrickman wears a special safety harness that enables him to lean out from the work platform (called the monkey board) to reach the drill pipe in the center of the derrick or mast and to throw a line around the pipe and pull it back into its storage location until it is time to run the pipe back into the well. In terms of skill, physical exertion, and perceived danger, a derrickman has one of the most demanding jobs on the rig crew. In an emergency, the derrickman can quickly reach the ground by an escape line often called the Geronimo line.

I climbed on the elevators used to lift or lower the drill pipe and rode up to the platform for the derrickman, the monkey board. The board was about one hundred ten feet above the ground and about eighty-five feet above the rig floor. I wrestled the nine stands of drill collars—a "stand" being three connected drill collars—into the hole after the bit was screwed into the bottom of the first stand. The drill collars must be handled much differently from the regular drill pipe, as each stand must be tied off separately. It is dangerous because the derrickman at the time had to get out of his safety belt during this process. I weighed 120 pounds, while each stand of drill collars weighed about 7,500 pounds.

Once the last stand of drill collars was lowered into the well hole, I began with the regular stands of drill pipe. The derrickman's job is to latch what are called elevators around the drill pipe to lift the stand up off the rig floor so it can be screwed onto the previous stand. These are screwed together first by spinning them with a chain wrapped around the drill pipe, then tightening with huge tongs. The sections of drill stems are then lowered into the hole one stand at a time.

The elevators were coming up fast, and I signaled for the driller to stop. Then I latched the stand of drill pipe into the elevators and was lifted up so floor hands could screw it into the previous joint. That was contrary to normal procedure and was supposed to be done in one swift motion. The driller was not supposed to stop on my signal. After about two or three times of this, Dickerson figured out that I did not know what I was doing. He brought me down from the derrick to the rig floor for a chewing out and more directions. Then he sent me back up to continue.

The only reason he did not fire me was because the wheat harvest had come through a few weeks before and most workers had gone with the wheat harvest. This poor driller only had me and two floor hands on the crew, none with much experience. Since Buster had to do the best that he could with what he had to work with, he would give me all sorts of tips on how to squat down so I could catch the stands of drill pipes quickly and latch them as I stood up and the elevators moved on up into the derrick. If I missed a stand during a round trip of removing the drill string to replace a bit and return to drilling, he would make me climb down the ladder instead of bringing me down on the elevators.

Part of the ordeal of what was one of the worst days of my life was almost over when we got the final stand of drill pipe in the hole. The driller then asked me if the pump "was lined up to drill?" One of the derrickman's jobs, in addition to racking the pipe in the derrick, is being responsible for all the drilling mud flow. Mud is the drilling fluid that flows down inside the drill pipe at high pressure to the bit at the bottom of the hole and carries or washes the cuttings up outside the drill pipe. I looked off the back of the rig platform and there was this huge mud pump and it looked lined up to me and I gave him a thumbs up. We kept blowing nail vales until I figured out what he meant. Once I got the right valves open, after several wrong attempts, we were able to get the drilling mud flowing in through the drill pipe and down to the drill bit. My learning curve was perpendicular.

As the weeks evolved, Dickerson taught me to be one of the better derrickmen around. After that job, I worked derricks from Oklahoma to Utah. Milton Biggs, one of my high school classmates, worked on another shift on this rig. He was sixteen. Over the next several years and attending college at OU or East Central I worked as a derrickman in Standard, Lee C. Moore, Oil Well, and Clear View Ideco derricks, among others.

Bountiful, Utah to Offshore Rigs

In the summer of 1955, when I was eighteen, my cous-

23

in Theron Simpson and I were on a crew that moved a drilling rig owned by C & L Drilling Company from Oklahoma to Bountiful, Utah, north of Salt Lake City. We drilled one well on the edge of the Great Salt Lake, which turned out to be a dry hole. We then moved the drilling rig back to Oklahoma. I have fond memories of Utah. The food we had there was great and the large Mormon families who often came out to watch us work were extremely cordial and welcoming.

After this Utah trip, one of the crew members, Glen Trease, and I decided to seek our fortune on offshore rigs in the Gulf of Mexico. We took off for Louisiana in my 1952 Ford two-door sedan. We picked up a hitchhiker in Morgan City, Louisiana, who was trying to get back to his offshore job on a drilling platform. He got us on board the drilling company boat to his rig about forty miles out in the Gulf. They served us lunch but were not hiring, so we returned to the dry land. We were traveling light and sleeping in my car.

After we got back to shore, Glen and I went to New Orleans for a couple of days. Having grown up in dry Oklahoma, I had never seen anything like Bourbon Street. We were able to get roughneck jobs on a land rig in Louisiana for a few days but did not care for the location. It was hot and sticky and full of mosquitoes. We decided to return to Ada, and I returned to college. That was a big turning point in my life, as I might never have gone back to college had I been hired on the offshore rig.

Oklahoma was dry back then, meaning hard liquor was illegal. We could not buy 3.2 beer which was legal but as teenagers we could buy hard liquor from bootleggers or anyone with a yellow porchlight. On occasion on the deep wells, if the driller or crew chief ran a Hughes brand drill bit, he got a pint of whisky from that bit salesman or if a Reed Drill bit he might get a pint of whiskey from that company. There were times we passed around a bottle at 7AM, for example while driving back to Ada from the morning tour (pronounced tower) shift seventy miles or so away and I still went to day class at East Central State College in Ada. My only D in college was from an early morning class in "Social and Square Dancing" which I seldom made in time. I often joke about growing up in the Bible belt where drinking and dancing was a sin. I have finally mastered drinking but am still working on dancing.

Tom Biggs, a driller for Kingery Drilling Company, was the uncle of my boyhood pals Wayne and Milton (Cub) Biggs. His perpetual crew for a couple of years for drilling oil wells near Ada consisted of Wayne, as Derrickman, Cub, my brother Tom, my cousin Theron Simpson, and me as his two floor hands as needed.

After getting out of the Army at age twenty, I went back to the University of Oklahoma in Norman—this time majoring in mechanical engineering. At that time, there were oil wells being drilled on many ten-acre locations on what was then known as the Norman Naval Base, now the OU south campus. Having little or no money, I would go out and work a full two weeks, having four overtime days on a drilling rig. Then I would quit and hit the books like crazy. Then I would go back for another two weeks.

Hard Banding Drill Pipe

When I was about 18 years old, I worked several weeks for a man named Foster Eaton. He was the husband of my high school typing teacher, Marcene Eaton. He had a truck-mounted piece of equipment with which he could hard-band drill pipe. What this involved was running several beads of weld around joints on the drill pipe used on oil-field drilling rigs. With this, the pipe twisting in the hole would not wear as much at the joints where the pipe was screwed together.

We worked on several projects in Texas and Oklahoma. Foster was quite a womanizer and an alcoholic. He would be missing for several days at a time while I drove the truck to the next job in another state. Then he would show up and we would finish the project.

Steam Rig

At age 19, I worked for a driller, or crew chief, named Bruce Russell. He had been a friend of my granddad's and was in his sixties at the time. I worked on one well for him at Fittstown, Oklahoma, as a derrickman. A brief time later we were tasked to rig up a steam-powered rig near Colgate, Oklahoma, to drill a saltwater disposal well for Robertson Drilling Corporation. There probably had not been a steam rig in the United States in the previous forty years.

We assembled this one from junk that had not been used in years. It was powered by four boilers and was just the reverse of the technology on the normal rotary drilling rigs. We had to use large pipe wrenches to keep the steam lines tightened. The rig was noticeably quiet; it would run almost silently sometimes but then sounded like a freight train the rest of the time. It was a wonderful experience that few will ever have.

Water Well Drillers

When I was nineteen and my younger brother Tom was seventeen, we put together a rotary drilling rig mounted on the back of a truck to drill water wells. We were assisted in this endeavor by a neighbor, Gus Graham, who was a welder. We assembled all the parts and pumps and a derrick and mounted them on a truck. For a couple of years, we drilled many water wells in and around Ada.

At one point we were approached by Concho Construction Company, a company that was doing a major construction project for Ideal Cement Company in Ada, Oklahoma. They had dug a huge pit in the ground to dump the limestone to make cement from but unfortunately needed to make it about 10 or 12 feet wider. My brother and I were hired to drill shot holes with our water well drilling rig every so many feet along the edge of this pit. Then they would place explosives in these holes and ignite them. It blew the rock and debris into the pit where they could more easily scoop it out. Since this was a union project, the contractor had us become members of the Operating Engineers Union.

My Last Day in the Oil Patch

When I was still working in the oil fields, and attending OU, a driller named Loren Groom would always hire me back because I was good at what I did. I had been on the Oklahoma City Police Department about two years, and one night, while on the 3PM to 11PM shift, I happened to be in the police station when a couple of officers brought him in. His wife had signed a complaint for being drunk and disorderly or I could have sprung him at once. After he was booked in, I went up to the jail on the top floor of the Police Station. The old guy was drunk, crying, and claiming he had to get to work at 11PM or he would lose his job. I learned that he had been demoted to a roughneck or floor hand from driller or crew chief. I asked where he was working, and he replied that he was working on a drilling rig running at SE 15th and Sunny Lane, only about two miles from the police station. I told him not to worry; I would take care of it.

I asked the Lieutenant to let me off 30 minutes early. I rushed home and grabbed my hard hat and steel-toe shoes and made his eight-hour shift. None of the others on the crew knew I was a police officer, just a friend of Loren. At the end of the shift, with no one injured, I signed his name. He got the overtime day pay, and I went to my day class. My last day in the oil patch as a roughneck was for free, and I was proud to have helped Loren keep his job.

Oklahoma City Police Department

I treasure my service on the Oklahoma City Police Department (OCPD) and the many friends I have from that era. It left a lasting impression. Occasionally, someone asks, "What was the most rewarding job you ever had, among all those diverse career paths?" My reply, "The opportunity to have served as a uniformed officer on the Oklahoma City Police Department in the late 1950s and early 1960s."

We saw the results of our work. It was immediate and in one's face. We made life-and-death decisions on the spot, decisions that often take courts several years to sort out. We caught the burglar in the building or robber in the act. We got the pregnant woman to the hospital before she had her baby in our police car, and we got the drunk driver off the street before he killed himself or someone else. We got the young child from a terribly bad home environment to safety at the shelter. We served as marriage counselors in our early twenties at domestic disturbance calls. We lived life to the fullest, worked nights, attended college full time during the day, worked extra jobs, and still found time to do what we wanted. We made more arrests in a month than I made in eight years with the FBI. We single officers were on the front lines to protect and serve when Helen Gurley Brown wrote Sex and the Single Girl, which started the sexual revolution.

We officers had more excitement in any one week than many people have in a lifetime. We engaged in high-speed chases, minus TV news choppers overhead. We learned to deal with people—when to push, and when to back off. We had unparalleled camaraderie, not seen since, with our then brother officers who always had our backs.

We had wonderful lieutenants and sergeants in the Scout Car Division. Lieutenant Ace Williams and Sergeant Walter Kostick were outstanding men, as was Sam Watson. There was little that Lieutenant Williams had not seen or experienced. He was the fatherly figure who treated us as the kids we were. He was in his mid-forties, and we thought he was old. At lineup or roll call, as we stood there with our partners at the start of the shift, he would read instructions about checking this or that and about high burglary rates, and then he would get to the subject of "sleeping." We were all going to school during the day or else working extra jobs, so a lot of dozing went on when there was little activity on the streets. "Men, when I was your age," he told us, "I never slept on the number three shift because I always had a hard-on so big (dream on, Ace!), I did not have enough skin left to close my eyes." He was known to catch officers asleep in their patrol car, perhaps in an alley. He would pull his cruiser within about two inches of their bumper, then call them on the radio to meet cruiser one (him) at some location immediately. They would be awakened by the call, slam the car in reverse, and bang into his car. He would have a big laugh, and they at least would not park or sleep again in that location. He would often say, "Shake a hand when you can." He encouraged us to treat the citizenry nicely. Once in the days when an outside spotlight was on police cars, Lieutenant Williams was chasing a car and shooting with his left hand. He shot out his spotlight.

I had never thought about becoming a police officer. They say that "luck trumps smarts every time," and I have been incredibly lucky. I had gotten off active duty with the Army in 1957 and started back to the University of Oklahoma in 1958, having attended a semester there in 1954. I was in the engineering school, had little or no money, and lived off and on with an aunt and uncle in Norman. As I related before, there were oil field drilling rigs next to the campus, and I would go out and pick up a derrickman job on a drilling rig and work a full two weeks on the 11PM to 7AM shift. Then I would quit and hit the books like crazy. Then do it all over again when the money ran out.

My boyhood friend Charlie Dyer lived on a farm near where I grew up. After a stint in the Army as a military policeman, he had joined the Oklahoma City Police Department and later rode motorcycles in the traffic division. Charlie asked me why I was killing myself on drilling rigs working seven days a week. He suggested I get on the police department with him. He told me that they had several guys on the department who were going to college and that they only worked six days a week. My question was, "Where do I sign?" Anything beat milking cows or working in the oil fields at that point in my life. Of course, he did not tell me up front that he meant that they worked 26 days in a row and then received four days off.

Deputy Chief Ed Rector told me when I reported for duty that they knew I would not stay for a career, but that they expected that we college guys would not get them in trouble while there. It was a good thing that he never knew about the many close calls we would have.

When I started at OCPD, I was paid $295 per month. When I left after three years, I was making $357 per month, plus a $75 per year uniform allowance, from which I paid my college tuition.

The first few weeks as a new officer, and before attending the next police academy, I worked with an experienced officer and a detective buying liquor and women as an undercover operative. When Oklahoma legalized liquor in 1960 there were still about eighty pending cases that had not yet gone to trial for possession or sale by bootleggers. They tried one of my cases as a test case. We lost, so all the remaining cases were dismissed. I also remember going out with "Salty Meals," the homicide guy at the time, to fingerprint stiffs in morgues. This was unnerving for one not accustomed to holding hands with dead bodies.

One of the more memorable classes I had during recruit school was taught by Dillinger-era FBI Agent Weldon "Spot" Gentry. Spot had a pot belly and would never have made the FBI weight program as I later knew it. He taught a six-hour block of instructions on when to use deadly force and when not to. He summed up his block with this teaching point: "Boys, remember, if someone is going to be buried and someone is going to get tried, make sure you are the one who is tried." He then walked out of the classroom. I will never forget that. Fortunately, I never had to shoot anyone, or else missed the ones we did shoot at—fleeing cars, burglars in buildings, etc.

After the Police Academy phase, I picked up a few hours of college credit at Oklahoma City University. I was assigned to the patrol or Scout Car Division. During my first year I rode with several partners, each of whom taught me a lot about police work.

I returned to classes at Oklahoma University in the fall of 1959 and commuted with two other scout-car officers who were in law school, Bob Macy, and Ray LeGrande. They were my inspiration to enter and finish law school.

After another semester at OU, I was tired of school and had almost enough hours for a degree in math and physics. I transferred to Central State, now the University of Central Oklahoma (UCO), in Edmond, where most of the other officers were attending. Several of us including Barbara Bobo, one of the stenographers who also worked night shifts, would commute to Edmond for 8AM classes at OCU after getting away from the Police Department by 7:30AM. Barbara would often drive while we guys rotated at stoplights to the back seat to get out of our uniforms. This was my fourth college—each of which I left in good standing academically. I finally obtained a math and physics degree in 1961.

Code 3, Red Light, and Siren

Around 1960 Oklahoma City expanded from fifty-seven square miles to 457 square miles in one day by annexing the suburbs. These were tumultuous times and we had three chiefs of police during my three years. Oklahoma City suddenly became the largest city in the nation in area. Some districts went from ten square miles to one hundred square miles or more with a whole host of different challenges. In addition to all the usual calls about domestic relations and car accidents, there were calls related to rural areas such as "a hawk getting a lady's chickens." We often ran red-light-and siren through Bethany, War Acres, Midwest City, and other communities to get to our emergency calls in our additional territory, ones formerly handled exclusively by the sheriff's department.

Tear Gassing New Citizens

Once I was riding with Henry Jones, who usually rode three wheelers writing parking tickets. We received a call in Green Acres, a newly annexed minority community in the far northeast part of the city. The police dispatcher reported someone was wielding a shotgun and threatening a man at a house there. We arrived at the same time as a Deputy Sheriff Jim Farris. A large crowd had congregated on a small rise about one hundred feet downwind from the house. The gunman had let his victim go by the time we arrived but was still in the house with a shotgun. Farris and I charged into the house to find that the gunman had taken refuge in the attic.

Being tall, I pushed up the trap door to the attic with my five-cell flashlight while Farris lobbed a military-strength tear gas grenade into the opening. (Where did he get that? I was impressed). Suddenly the gunman stomped his way through the drywall ceiling and dropped to the floor, where we handcuffed him. The tear gas was smoking and steaming from the cedar shingles on the roof and blowing downwind to the 20 to 30 new Oklahoma City residents and spectators, all of whom were heavily gassed. I was gassed myself when I had to retrieve the shotgun from the attic.

During this apprehension, Jones initially did not get out of the car. I did not think Jones was a reliable partner for me at the time. I had expected someone who could be counted upon to back me up, but maybe he was just a lot smarter than me or Farris and wanted to be able to go home to his family after the shift.

Shot Through Picture Window

One night around midnight, Officer Dale Harbolt fired a shot at a burglar at 23rd and North Shartel. A brief time later, my partner and I received a call to 36th and Shartel, a mile away. Upon arrival, we found that the bullet from Dale's .357 Magnum had knocked a hole in the picture window of a home, making about a 4-inch hole due to the round's trajectory and diminished velocity. The homeowner never knew the source of the bullet. We had to buy our own weapons at the time, so many of us opted for the more powerful magnums.

Shot Through Police Car Windshield

Hershel Baker was riding with Ben Caswell one night when they were summoned to an armed robbery of Byron Gambulos' liquor store. Baker was in the passenger seat and became so excited that he accidentally fired his gun through the police car windshield as they pulled up. I understand that he had to pay for the windshield.

Car Accidents

I was riding solo to an emergency call a week or so after we had gotten the new fleet of 1960 Fords. I was going north on Shartel just two blocks from the police station at about sixty miles per hour in a 25-miles-per-hour zone when a car ran a stop sign, and I demolished the first of the new fleet. I was never so happy to see a drunk driver, as I was way over the 10-mile-per-hour above the speed limit that we were authorized. The drunk was just shaken up. I, however, received two parallel gashes in the top of my head from the screws on the cap badge when my head hit the ceiling. Seat belts? We don't wear no stinking seat belts! The lieutenant was off that night, and I went to Army Reserve Summer Camp the next day. Two weeks later, when I returned, a couple of others from the new car fleet had been wrecked, so my butt chewing was not as bad as it could have been.

As new officers were hired, we old timers of two years took them on to expose them to the real world. During one of those periods when Royce Hodges and I were split up to ride with new trainees, Royce had new officer Chuck Stanfill, who went on to a career in the bureau of Alcohol, Tobacco, and Firearms, and I had Melvin Kiesel, who later would retire from the El Paso Police Department. We had our two scout cars in the same district one night when we received a prowler call. We would often run with our lights off in these situations. I came in fast and went past the address. I slammed the car in reverse and began flying backwards, not being able to see or know that Royce was coming in behind me, also with no lights. The press report mentioned that officer George's foot slipped off the clutch, an understatement or fabrication.

Armed Robbery on Northeast 23rd Street

My partner Royce Hodges and I covered the then District Four in Oklahoma City, which ran from Santa Fe East and from 13th Street North. We received a call about an armed robbery on Northeast 23rd Street, which was a part of our new district. The armed robbery had occurred at a liquor store on Northeast 23rd Street, north of Tinker Air Force Base. Two robbers had gone in the front of the store to rob the wife, who was at the counter. The husband, who was in the back room, saw what was going on. He grabbed a shotgun and went out the back door and came around outside the building. When the robbers came out the front, he shot one of them and one got away. The temperature was in the 20s, and when we arrived this body was lying there steaming and oozing blood. We presumed that he was dead.

We went on about our duties of taking information and getting out a radio report to try to find the other robber. After about ten minutes of this, I noticed that the "dead" robber moved. I told Royce, "I think this old boy's still alive; we better call an ambulance." Such was the life of first responders in the sixties.

Firearm Discharges

I had Robert Wilder as a trainee during his first month on the police department. He had been a clerk in the FBI Office until he became old enough for the police department where his father had once served. We received a call to a southside neighborhood to find that the commotion was caused by a possum about forty feet up in a tree. Dogs were barking and about twenty neighbors had congregated. Upon assessing the situation, trainee Wilder pulled out his service revolver and shot the possum at the top of the tree in the darkness, which was impressive to me. It fell onto the street and the dogs stopped barking. I could not help but wonder what bad press we would have gotten if he had missed. Bob Wilder would later go to the FBI National Academy at my urging and become chief of police. He retired as the sheriff in Marshall County at Madill, Oklahoma, and died shortly thereafter from a fall at home.

Another time I was riding alone on the day shift when I received a call on East Reno, near what is now Brick Town. A man was taking a large hog to the slaughterhouse when the hog escaped from his low trailer. It was running about the intersection disrupting traffic and wreaking havoc. Unable to corral the animal, its owner asked for my service revolver and then shot the hog in the head. We were then able to load the carcass back into the trailer and restore traffic. You do what you must do at the moment.

Extra Jobs

Being a police officer was not a high-paid job, and we each worked other jobs for extra income as these would become available. There was work in private security at events. I worked at Mercy and St. Anthony Hospital emergency rooms off and on. The hospital management wanted an off-duty officer at the emergency room at night. Normally we would just sleep on a gurney in a side room. We would be awakened if a particular problem occurred such as a drunk or unruly patient or a gunshot victim appearing at the emergency room.

For two Christmas seasons, I worked at the post office delivering packages. We drove Army three-quarter ton vehicles loaned to the Post Office. The person in charge of vehicles at the time preferred off duty police officers for safety and reliability concerns with his temporary package delivery positions.

About a year into my stint with the police department I was riding solo on the day shift when dispatched to a bar on North Western Avenue. Upon arrival I found an unconscious, older white male turning slightly blue and lying on the bar floor. He was surrounded by a dozen or so other bar patrons all staring down at him. Upon seeing me, they began loudly demanding I take him to the hospital. Avoiding a potential riot, I hustled the guy into the front seat of my patrol car with the help of some patrons. I departed code three to Mercy Hospital about a mile away. It was common at that time to transport patients to the hospital in our police cars due to a lack of better options. About a block before reaching the hospital, I passed an ambulance going in the opposite direction, headed to the same bar.

After getting my passenger into the emergency room for a quick examination, he was pronounced dead. As it turned out he had choked on a sausage, probably a Vienna sausage. These were often provided to patrons from a large jar set on the bar. The basic first-aid training at the police academy at that time did not cover much more than stopping bleeding or delivering babies. Even if I had recognized the problem, the Heimlich maneuver was not known back then. It may have already been too late upon my arrival at the bar, but it troubled me that perhaps had I received better first aid training I might have immediately recognized what was wrong and saved the fellow. I signed up for a Red Cross first-aid course on my own. Afterwards, among other things I might need on the shift such as flashlight batteries, note pads, etc., I always carried a crooked plastic device in my AWOL bag

I carried in my scout car. This device could be pushed down a victim's throat to clear any obstruction.

Roommate at OCPD

As an aside, my roommate through much of my OCPD service was Bill Bruce, who went on from OCPD to complete college at Central State and to become head of security there. He later was a deputy sheriff and then a prosecutor, an assistant attorney general, and assistant commissioner of Oklahoma's Department of Public Safety. I had the honor to sit at the counsel table in the U.S. Supreme Court with him once when he argued a case there as an assistant attorney general for Oklahoma (the closest I ever came to having a case there). I was in Oklahoma for a visit when his first wife Della and baby died in childbirth. He was in shambles from this tragedy, as one would expect. I asked what he planned to do. He told me that he and his wife had talked about his going to law school that fall, but that was now out of the question. Wrong. I took him directly from the burial at the cemetery to Oklahoma City University and enrolled him in OCU law school.

Military Deserters

While with the OCPD I had a source who would provide me and my partner Royce Hodges lists of military deserters possibly in Oklahoma City. We picked up several while scouting around at night. We would take them to Tinker Air Force Base, where we got a $25 reward. This knowledge came in handy later when I was an FBI Agent in Lynchburg, Virginia.

Willie Pep's Ex-Wife

My partner Royce Hodges and I received a call on an attempted suicide. I do not recall how it was reported to the police dispatcher or by whom. In any event, we picked up the alleged victim whom I recall as being a small person and took her to Mercy Hospital. She claimed to be an ex-wife of a featherweight boxer named Willie Pep. At the emergency room she had her stomach pumped from an overdose of pills. We put her back in the police car to drive her back to where she was living. We were both joking with her that we bet it was kind of an unpleasant experience to have one's stomach pumped, and that she would not try that again. Suddenly she rummaged around in her purse, came out with another bottle of pills, and swallowed them. We had to make a U-turn and take her back to the hospital and have her stomach pumped out the second time.

Let's Look for Us

My partner, the late Royce Hodges, and I were having affairs with a couple of babes. Mine was dating the then perpetual Lt. Governor Nigh, single at the time (she said all he wanted to do was talk about Oklahoma). The other was dating one of his friends. Both were legal secretaries with Pierce Malk (phonetic) and Duncan law firm. After midnight, the guys would drop off the gals at their apartment just north of NW 23rd, whereupon Royce and I might get a call to come by if we were available. We would report out of the car for dinner, put our blue nylon raincoats on over our uniforms, and go in for a therapy session (protect and serve). One night when we went back in service (from some public service) we got a call that somebody at that very apartment house had called the police department to complain that periodically vandals were turning out the lights in the apartment hallway late at night. I said to Royce, "Come on. Let's drive around and look for us."

Like that Honey

One officer who would later go to Alcohol, Tobacco, and Firearms (ATF) was allegedly having sex in the back seat of his patrol car on one of the many oil leases scattered throughout the city. Reportedly, the story goes, after he was spent, his lady friend tapped him on the back, pointed up at the oil well pump jack going up and down, and said "like that honey."

Boys, Please Take Me

One night at about 2AM, Royce and I got a call to a residence in upper Northeast Oklahoma City to deal with a domestic disturbance. The husband, a banker, had come home with the proverbial lipstick on his collar, and they had a loud fight—loud enough that the neighbors called. Once inside the house we separated the parties, with Royce talking to the wife, and me the husband. As it turned out, he was the cousin of a banker in my hometown of Ada. He whispered to me, "Boys, please take me." So, we hustled him out of the house and put him in the back of the police car. We had nothing to charge him with, so we took him to a nearby motel and checked him in. About 4AM we were napping on an oil lease when all hell broke loose with calls from the lieutenant. Seems wifey reconsidered. She and her high-priced lawyer showed up at the jail to bail him out, but he was not there. We had to go roust the poor guy out of bed and get him back home. He probably got less sleep than we did.

Next Steps

As I mentioned before, I had finished at Central State in January 1961 with my B.S. degree in math and physics. In August 1961, Kenneth Gee, a fellow officer, and classmate at UCO, told me that the FBI was now hiring science majors with prior law enforcement experience. He had applied but was rejected due to a medical issue. I contacted the local FBI office and made an application. I was also in the Army Reserve, and that same month, I received a direct commission as a second lieutenant in the Military Police Corps from my MP Unit with the 95th Infantry Division in Oklahoma City. I also started at the Oklahoma City University Law School.

The FBI conducted a background check over the next few months, after which I was called by the Local FBI Office and informed that they wanted me to take a physical at Tinker Air Force Base. I told the agent that I was on my days off so this would be a suitable time to do it. He told me to be there at 7:30AM the following morning. About fifteen minutes later I received another call from the agent to the effect that they were booked up and could not take me for another month.

My next call was to my drinking/skirt-chasing buddy, Paul Nelson. Paul's mother owned the tow truck service that the police department used in Northeast Oklahoma City. He was the administrator of the Tinker Air Force Base Hospital. When he answered, I asked him why it took a month to get a physical for the FBI at his "[expletive deleted]" hospital. He asked why I wanted a physical. I told him it was for the FBI. He told me to be there at 7:30AM the following morning. I told him to call the FBI back and tell him there was a cancellation. Another fifteen minutes passed, and I received a third call from this FBI agent who handled recruiting. He was extremely excited. He said, "Oh Mr. George, the most wonderful thing happened. They called to tell me they had a cancellation, and to be there tomorrow." I told him I would be there. Paul walked me through all the stages, and I was finished in thirty minutes. What I did not know at the time was that if there were any delays, I might have missed the new agent training class for which I was slated. If there were later budget cuts, which often happened, I might never have gotten the job. Timing is important.

OCPD in The Big Apple

Another time my wife and I were staying at the PepsiCo corporate apartment at the Marriott on Central Park in Manhattan. I had just started my law practice, and PepsiCo was sending a car to take me up to headquarters in Purchase, New York, so that I could hustle some business from my former FBI friends (and now officials) there. The plan was to drop Nancy off at one of the Manhattan department stores on the way. She and I were standing outside the hotel waiting for our ride when I noticed Ed Atkinson and his wife coming down the street toward us. Ed was still on the Oklahoma City Police Department. He was in New York city with his wife for a convention connected to her business. Ed and I were in the same recruit class. We were standing there talking about what a small world to run into friends from OKC on the streets of New York when the doorman announced, "Mr. George, your car is ready." I looked around to observe one of the biggest, longest limousines I had ever seen. I said, "It's been great to see you," and we got in the limo and drove off with them gaping at us. If I had planned and rehearsed it, this could not have been better.

J. Edgar Hoover's FBI

In early January 1962, while I was still with the Oklahoma City Police Force, I worked from 11PM to 7AM each day. One day, right after my shift ended, I called the FBI office to ask about the status of my application—only to be told they had sent me a telegram two weeks earlier. It was sent to the wrong address by the meticulous FBI. I had three days to get from Oklahoma City to Washington, D.C., and this was before the interstate highway system. I checked out of the Police Department during the day, sold my uniforms, and cleaned out my apartment. By 6PM that evening I was driving toward Washington, D.C. in my 1961 Ford Convertible. I made a stop at the no-tell motel on the way out of town for a goodbye to the head of the State Crime Bureau's daughter.

I arrived in our nation's capital, completely exhausted, late on the night before my New Agents Class was slated to begin in the Old Post Office Building, now the Waldorf Astoria. I was without any suit, the required gray pants and white shirt, and the uniform fedora.

Quantico

The FBI Academy, when I was there in the 1960s, was located on the main base at Quantico. A few years later a new complex was constructed near the firing range west of Quantico. The FBI Academy courses rotated between D.C. and Quantico for the next twelve weeks with most classroom work in D.C. and the firing range and physical training at Quantico. One of my New Agent class members dropped out for family reasons, but the rest of us passed with flying colors, and we met the director. There were only two lawyers in our class. Most of us were former police and military.

Our 12-week course consisted of classroom work on laws involving cases the FBI investigated, firearms, and physical training. I became a highly effective shooter with great training by professionals, though happily I never had to shoot anyone.

At one of the specialty ranges, Hogan's Alley, where good guys and bad guys would pop up in a window, I shot both the FBI agent and the kid, which got me some ribbing from my classmates. I was just following Spot Gentry's advice from the OCPD police academy to make sure I was the one getting tried and not buried.

At Quantico, I thought I had died and gone to heaven. I was sleeping in a bed instead of a police car, eating three meals a day, and making more money than my former chief of police. I gained twenty-four pounds.

"FBI CRACK POTS"

My first office assignment with the FBI was at the Richmond, Virginia, Field Office. I was there for several months and handled general criminal and applicant matters before being transferred to Lynchburg, Virginia, as the resident agent. Early on, I was sent temporarily to the Alexandria, Virginia Resident Agency and to other places in Virginia to help as needed or fill in for some agent on vacation.

In Alexandria, I worked on a matter involving Clive

Rigdon. He had a large house trailer that he towed behind his old Cadillac. The trailer and the back of his car were covered with all kinds of derogatory remarks about the FBI and other federal agencies. He brought this charade to Washington, D.C. periodically. FBI Headquarters wanted him surveilled so they would know when he might be coming back into the District of Columbia. His colorful trailer made quite a spectacle as he ran up and down Pennsylvania Avenue. He would camp out in the Virginia Shenandoah mountains for a while, then return to the District of Columbia. There was no such thing as a discreet surveillance on one-lane country roads in the Shenandoah Valley where he might park for a few days. Some of the agents were jerks and would throw rocks at his trailer. I, on the other hand, would chat with him at night standing between his old Cadillac and his trailer, and my bureau car a few hundred feet down the road. He called me "Anonymous Joe," as I would not give him my name.

I finally understood what his beef with the FBI and other government agencies was all about. He had been a machinist in a defense plant. After World War II was over, everyone was stealing stuff from the plant. He kept reporting this to the authorities and eventually was fired, for which he blamed government agencies. I told him to stop acting like a nut, to get his material together, and to see his Senator. Days later we surveilled him to Capitol hill, where he had driven in his old Cadillac sedan. He had left the trailer across the river in Virginia. He waved to me as he entered the Senate Office Building with a stack of papers under his arm. We never heard from him again. Some matters can be resolved by just listening.

The Lynchburg Resident Agency (RA) was normally a two-man agency or office. Jack Freeze, who was the other FBI agent assigned to this RA, had been there since World War II. He had medical problems and back problems, which kept him out much of the time during the period I was there. As a result, I was, for all practical purposes, the lone "Fed" in a one-man RA in my first field office. Having been a police officer, and having been a military police officer, I did fine with the locals. I was responsible for territory that included the City of Lynchburg and the five surrounding counties of Amherst, Appomattox, Bedford, Buckingham, and Campbell. Much of the investigative work there involved general criminal leads and apprehending military deserters.

It seemed that some service men from that part of the country would dock in Norfolk, Virginia, with their ship, come home to chop a supply of wood for the family for the winter, and forget to go back to the ship. As a result, they would be declared "absent without leave." After they were AWOL more than 30 days, they were declared "deserters," and their case would be turned over to the FBI. Having been a former police officer in Oklahoma City, I knew the drill quite well in apprehending deserters. Police officers could get a reward from the government of $25 for each apprehension when they returned a deserter to military control. This reward, I understood, came out of the salary of the individual deserter.

Federal agents, of course, were not eligible for this bounty. I, however, made many friends in my RA territory with both the State Police and the Lynchburg Police Department. Any time that I had to apprehend a military deserter I would take a local police officer or state trooper with me. They would log the deserter into the nearest jail, qualifying for the reward. We would notify the military service to come get them. I would then report the apprehension to FBI Headquarters, and I got credit there.

Still, there was a rift at the time between the FBI and local law enforcement. The FBI was perceived to be too secretive, and this was the civil rights era in the South. The FBI investigated civil rights cases, which sometimes involved acts of local law officers, so many were a bit skeptical. I had prior law enforcement experience, and the locals appreciated it. I shared all the information I could with them, and they reciprocated with great support to me personally. FBI agents who had been former police officers were precluded from working civil rights cases. It was a blessing on one hand and perhaps discrimination against us former police officers on the other hand.

I happened to be in the Amherst County, Virginia, Courthouse late one afternoon. A Virginia State Trooper had two boys in custody who had stolen a car and transported it across state lines. Normally, the state police handled these matters, but the trooper was disgusted with his job that day and was stuck with booking these fellows. He wanted to go home on time. I told him I was happy to take them off his hands. He said, "If you do that, when would you take them?" I replied, "I will take them right now. Loan me a pair of handcuffs." I handcuffed one suspect's left wrist to the right wrist of the other suspect and placed them in the back seat of the bureau car and buckled the seatbelt around both. I told them I would have to shoot them if they moved and took off for Lynchburg. I got credited for two more felony apprehensions and allowed the trooper to go home for dinner with his family.

Another time, near Appomattox, I passed an abandoned car with an out of state license plate beside the highway. About a quarter of a mile later I found two boys walking away from this car. I stopped and identified them, then radioed the Virginia State Police Headquarters at Appomattox, my dispatcher. Bureau Cars in Virginia only had state-police radios back then in outlying areas. The state police dispatcher checked and indicated that no one had any warrants on either of them, or there were no reports of the car having been reported stolen. I had to let them loose. A couple of days later, a stolen car report finally came in from West Virginia. I had the suspects already identified and matched with the car. Once I went back to the neighborhood, I spoke with a farmer in the field nearby who told me that he had observed the boys leaving the car and then me talking to them later a distance away. That made the case, and I received a Letter of Commendation from Mr. Hoover. I do not know if or when they were later apprehended and charged, but they had been identified by me, and we had recovered the vehicle.

On another occasion, while headed out to cover a lead in one of my counties, I came across an abandoned, and later reported to be missing, 18-wheeler tractor trailer with a load of liquor. The driver had apparently decided to unseal the cargo and take a case or two for himself. He became drunk, abandoned the truck, and the truck and contents were reported missing. Recovering the truck with about $100,000 worth of cargo blew the Theft from Interstate Shipment statistics far out of sync with previous years for the Richmond FBI office. It had never had a recovery of that magnitude. The office then needed to exceed that statistic the following year to remain in good graces with FBI Headquarters.

Captain Dennis Robertson

As an aside, one of the Lynchburg Police Officers whom I worked with was Dennis Wayne Robertson. He was married and had a couple of young daughters. He seemed a cut above some of his coworkers, and I suggested that he go with the Virginia State Police (VSP). That job paid more and had more prestige. He indicated that he had gone into the Army and had not finished high school. The State Police required that one be a high school graduate. I told him "No problem." I was having a fling with the gal who handled GED tests in Lynchburg. Dennis would come over to my apartment Saturday mornings and we worked the high school equivalency tests until he completed his degree. I had known the gals in the front office of the VSP while I was assigned in Richmond. His application stayed on top of the stack, and he was promptly hired. Dennis went on to hold nearly every job in the Virginia State Police except the head of it. Each time he got another promotion he would call to thank me. He retired as a captain with 44 years of law enforcement service. Fifty years later, he would expedite my New Mexico Bar application paperwork when a statement from the VSP was needed for the National Conference of Bar Examiners.

Field Office Inspections

The FBI inspection team had a reputation as people who should be avoided at all costs. An inspector's aide came to the Lynchburg RA during the annual field office inspection while I was there as the only agent. It was unusual that an FBI agent in his first office was assigned as an RA by himself. The inspector was Hobson H. Adcock, and he would later become a great mentor and coach. His inspection mission was to determine what we did at the Lynchburg RA and to review progress on various cases on which we were working. I had a wide variety of cases from criminal, such as bank robberies to background checks for federal officials. I also took him to meet the local police chief to confirm we were getting along there. All of this I passed with flying colors. Adcock said that if I ever came to Washington, D.C. I should stop by FBI headquarters. He would be pleased to introduce me to key officials. He gave me a considerable amount of career advice during his day in Lynchburg, which was to benefit me many-fold in later years.

A few months later, I received a transfer to Newark, New Jersey. Whether Adcock intended me to do so or not, I dropped by FBI headquarters on the way and visited my new friend the inspector. He introduced me to Assistant Director Cartha (Deke) DeLoach and to Helen Gandy, Mr. Hoover's personal secretary. He also introduced me to other front office personnel in the Crime Records Division. This division was the Public Relations arm of FBI Headquarters. I would later work directly with these people in Atlantic City and later at PepsiCo, when DeLoach became VP for Public Affairs.

Newark Field Office and Atlantic City

In the Newark field office, I was assigned to the squad that handled, among other federal crimes, Selective Service violators and interstate theft of motor vehicles. Occasionally, I would be tasked to help in the organized crime area. For a farm boy from rural Oklahoma with an "Okie" accent, it was quite an experience and involved a bit of a language barrier when working on the docks in Hoboken and Jersey City. It turned out that I got along better than the natives. As soon as I flipped out the credentials and said, "FBI," the next question from some big, burly longshoreman or other person that I needed to talk to might be, "Where are you from?" Once I told them Oklahoma, as luck would have it, they might have been stationed at Fort Sill or Tinker Air Force base or knew someone who had been. That broke the ice, and we would get along fine. It was common to knock on doors in Jersey City and someone might stick their head out three floors up and yell, "What do you want?" and the reply would be "FBI. Want all your neighbors to know?" They would not want their neighbors to know, so they would rush down and respond at ground level at the doorway.

I had never experienced Chinese food until a day when I had a lead to cover at a Chinese restaurant in Jersey City. It seems that one of the cooks had jumped ship in the New York harbor years earlier and had never registered for the Selective Service. I purposely had lunch before I went by the restaurant to cover this lead. After arriving, it turned out that the owner had been an FBI informant during World War II. He loved the FBI and insisted on giving me the run of his Chinese restaurant. He set up a table with a white tablecloth in the kitchen and proceeded to ply me with all manner of Chinese delicacies I had never eaten before. I left quite stuffed and with a deep appreciation of Chinese cuisine.

We made an agreement allowing the cook to register with Selective Service the next day so I would not have to take him away from the kitchen. Most of these Selective Service violators were new immigrants who spoke little English, and if they were in fact drafted, they could never pass the entrance exam for the military anyway. For the several months that I was on that squad, I fell into a routine with Selective Service violators. Rather than going out and interviewing all these individuals who did not know that they were supposed to register for Selective Service, I would put them in my bureau car and drive them down to Selective Service office and register them. I knew that once they were registered, the U.S. attorney would decline prosecution, and I could close the case. This kept my statistics on closing cases at the maximum and allowed me to befriend several new immigrants.

On one memorable occasion, I went to pick up a young Puerto Rican kid in a public housing project in Newark. When I arrived at the apartment, his immediate family and extended family were there, along with a Catholic priest. The kid was dressed up in his very finest Sunday clothes, and all his family were dressed up. They thought since the FBI was coming to get him that this was probably the last time they would ever see him. Between me and the priest, we finally were able to convince the family that I would bring him back home in an hour. I found it quite comical. As with all the others, I took him down to the Selective Service office and registered and returned him to his grateful family. I probably still have friends there who admire the FBI.

In Newark, I enrolled in the Seaton Hall Law School

at night, as it was near the office, and I wanted to finish after my one semester at Oklahoma City University Law School. I had to leave for the FBI New Agents class from there. Three weeks later, an old-time Special Agent in Charge, SAC Ralph Bachman—who had caught Nazi saboteurs in World War II—learned of this. He called me into his office, told me that I was just trying to get another job (which was not true) and that he was not going to cooperate with me. He summarily transferred me to the Atlantic City RA. He did me a favor, as I would not have survived trying to complete law school at night in a small office where everyone must roll when some crisis occurs.

In Atlantic City we covered the southernmost counties of Atlantic, Cape May, and Cumberland. The senior resident agent there, Leo Clark, did not want me and was a real jerk. I had been foisted upon him against his will, as he did not want any single agents in his RA territory for reasons best known to him. He was perhaps thinking the social life of a single agent might cause him embarrassment. It was an eight-man office at the time, and I teamed up with fellow Agent John B. Meade, a tough New Yorker. We took no blowback from this twit and got the job done with no interference.

While I was in a bar in Atlantic City, it came over the TV that President Kennedy had just been assassinated. The bar owner, whom I was interviewing about a stolen car in his parking lot, became irate that I was not working the assassination. I reminded him that I had only learned about this when he did. The convention center in Atlantic City was a popular place for politicians speaking at conventions, and we were stuck on the President Lyndon Johnson protection detail on occasion until the

Secret Service was able to staff up after the Kennedy assassination.

Democratic Convention

I was a part of the "'special squad' of agents who could be counted upon to act with discretion on the president's behalf."[1] We worked the Democratic National Convention in 1964. Assistant Director Cartha DeLoach arrived from FBI headquarters and announced to us that we were there to protect the president, who was concerned that if any violence erupted it might cost him the election. Attorney General Bobby Kennedy was trying to wrest the nomination from LBJ. I was the fair-haired boy here, as I had met DeLoach, Adcock and the rest of the headquarters staff before.

My work was at the state police command post in Convention Hall. The Mississippi Freedom Democratic Delegation was trying to replace the regular Mississippi delegation. The burned car bodies from the dead civil rights workers from Mississippi were being hauled up and down Atlantic and Pacific Avenues with loudspeakers blaring. Most of the civil rights organizations at the time were trying to create disruptions to embarrass the president and were allied with Bobby Kennedy. We had wiretaps and surveillance on most of these groups and their leaders, including Martin Luther King. In addition, we had some undercover agents planted in the civil rights groups. All the info we were gathering was being beamed to Walter Jenkins and Bill Moyers on the LBJ Staff. They were directing us about who we needed to remove from the convention floor to limit the chaos. We had a lid on

1   *G-Man* by Beverly Gage (Penguin, 2023), p. 598

most of the activities adverse to LBJ, no doubt at Bobby Kennedy's expense, and no violence erupted. It was Democrat on Democrat, so this was apparently okay. I received a letter of commendation crediting me with demonstrating "exemplary technical skill."

Our now experienced Political Convention Team was alerted for the 1968 Democratic Convention in Chicago. We were not called up, with predictable results. To me, it was one of the worst abuses I had seen. In 1964, there were billboards on the boardwalk outside the convention hall on the ocean saying, "In your heart you know he is right. Vote for Barry Goldwater." Those billboards were very appealing to many of us.

Deke DeLoach and I were having lunch at his Country Club in Hilton Head, South Carolina, in 2008, shortly before he died. We were reminiscing about our experiences back in Atlantic City in 1964 with the Democratic Convention. We had only two of a handful of Black FBI Agents in the Bureau at the time. Both were working undercover with the civil rights groups that were allied with AG Bobby Kennedy that were stirring up demonstrations. Deke shared something I did not know at the time. One of our undercover agents was sleeping with the head civil rights gal, so we were getting great undercover intelligence on demonstrations and efforts to disrupt the convention. Deke said he told this Agent, "I just don't want to know."

Meeting Mr. Hoover

Hob Adcock, my inspector friend, had instructed me to ask to see the Director if I ever got the opportunity. Mr. Hoover prided himself on the fact that he had personally met each one of his then 6,000 special agents. What they did not tell was that he met everyone during new agents' classes. This was quite an experience. We each carried an extra clean white starched shirt to class for several days while on call for a time when our class might meet "the Director." Finally, we got the call, with 30 minutes notice, to go to FBI headquarters from the Old Post Office Building a block away. The twenty-eight agents in my class quickly filed in one door and out the other, shaking hands with Mr. Hoover in the process. Clyde Tolson, the number two person in the FBI at the time, was standing over in the background. As we later understood, if he received a signal from Mr. Hoover that someone did not make the right appearance or had a weak handshake or sweaty palm, or some other blemish, the signal was given to Tolson, and that person would be summarily dismissed from the class. Fortunately, we all survived.

However, when agents came back for in-service refresher training at D.C. and Quantico, they were given the option to indicate whether they wanted to see Mr. Hoover. He would be happy to meet with them for a longer session. It was a risky move, though, if he was not impressed. Some agents used the opportunity to plead for transfers—for example, if their child needed medical treatment in Boston or Houston.

Newark Special Agent in Charge Ralph Bachman called me to his office in Newark to let me know that I had been selected to attend in-service training in D.C. In the same breath he said, "I don't suppose you have any burning desire to see the Director, do you?" This was an effort to chill any interest for me. Special agents in charge were terrified that an agent would make some remark intentionally or unintentionally that might cause the special agent in charge to be fired or to receive some other grief, such as having the inspection staff descend upon his office. When Mr. Bachman—the agent who caught Nazi saboteurs in World War II and who transferred me to Atlantic City when he found I was going to law school—asked this, I replied, "Gee boss, I've been meaning to talk to you about that, because I would like to see the Director." He was not happy.

While in Washington for the training session, I was ushered into Mr. Hoover's office. Mr. Hoover was not very tall, and he sat behind the desk. He stood up to shake hands and offered me a seat beside his desk. I told him that I did not have any problems, was happy with my work, and I just wanted an opportunity to say hello (as I had been scripted). With that, Mr. Hoover spent the next 30 minutes talking about the early days of the FBI, the Karpus Gang, John Dillinger, et al. I did not get a chance to say anything further. Interestingly, the cushion in the chair I was sitting in was not over four inches above the floor. So, I am staring almost straight up, looking at Mr. Hoover (God himself) while he spoke. After my allotted time was up, his secretary buzzed, he stood up, shook hands, thanked me for coming in, and I left.

One special agent in charge was so rattled after one of these meetings with Mr. Hoover that he reportedly walked into the coat closet instead of out the exit door. He stayed in there for a while. When he finally exited the closet, Mr. Hoover said, "What kept you?"

As my inspector friend and career advisor had suggested, it was a good move. I was able later to get a copy of the memo that Mr. Hoover had added to my personnel file. It read: "Today I saw Special Agent George of the Newark Office. He makes a good appearance, he seems intently interested in his work, and he should be considered for administrative advancement." This meant that I could have progressed upward in the FBI had I stayed, and better yet, having the memo in the file from the director that I was a good agent and should be considered for advancement, kept any special agent in charge from saying that I was the biggest screw up that ever came through his field office.

The director was infallible. Once Mr. Hoover misspoke in Congressional testimony stating that all his agents received 14 weeks of training at the FBI Academy at Marine Corps Schools, Quantico, Virginia, when then they only received twelve 12 weeks of training. The current class going through at that time reportedly had to stay an extra two weeks. When Mr. Hoover testified before Congress that there were x number of wiretaps and y number of microphones in place on that day, the number was accurate at that moment, even though the night before agents may have been pulling some out to get to the number in the testimony. The next night they would be putting them back in.

If some kid threw a brick through a window down on 14th Street in D.C. or anywhere in the downtown area, bureau cars had to scramble to the director's house in pristine upper northwest, D.C., to patrol the area. We called it "Hoowatch." I doubt that the director was aware of this effort, which was probably authorized by some underling at FBI Headquarters. Mr. Hoover was an old Victorian gentleman who probably should have retired after World War II. No one criticized the old guy when he was alive. His files that got so much attention were, in fact, kept in a secure location so the agents would not leak stuff on Congresspeople and Senators, several of whom thought he had more on them than he did.

Washington Field Office

Along with twenty-one other single agents, I was transferred (we did not have family or kids in school that might
delay us) on one day's notice to the Washington Field
Office (WFO) for the "Walter Jenkins Special." President Johnson's aide Walter Jenkins was the one we had
been working closely with in Atlantic City four months
earlier at the Democratic Convention. He was caught
in a homosexual incident in the YMCA across from the
White House. Our special assignment was to do background checks on all the White House Staff. Being the
clever person he was, LBJ used this new requirement to
get rid of several Kennedy holdovers with drinking and
other problems that made them unfit to work there. Pri-
or to that time, background checks were not required at
the White House, although many employees may have
had one in a previous agency or the military.

Thanks to my Crime Records Divisions friends Deloach and Adcock at FBI Headquarters, I was the only
one of the twenty-one who came out of a resident agency, as it took two transfers to fill the vacancy from my departure, one to the field office headquarters and a second
one to an RA city. When the first opportunity came up,
my name was on the transfer list for WFO, and this was
it. They knew that I wanted to finish law school.

Once after doing a neighborhood background check,
I got back to my bureau car only to discover keys lying
on the front seat. I had locked myself out of the car. I
thought I might as well conduct another interview. So,
I knocked on another door. After my interview of that

resident—asking about the character, associates, reputation, and loyalty (CARL, we called it) of her White House staff neighbor—I asked this lady if I could borrow a wire coat hanger. Here I was, an FBI agent, breaking into an FBI car with all these neighbors I had just interviewed watching me do so.

For a time, I wore mostly lightweight and cheap suits designed for summer wear. I would wear thermal underwear underneath in the cold. I had to get in and out of the car and often go inside houses for interviews. It was just easier. Thus, I did not need to take a heavy topcoat off and on. One freezing day I knocked on a lady's door to interview her about a neighbor. The temperature was in the teens. When she answered the door and I identified myself as an FBI Agent, she exclaimed, "Young man, aren't you cold?" I said, "No ma'am, I have my thermal underwear on." She likely assumes all FBI agents wear thermal underwear all the time.

It is good to have friends in the right places. As an agent in the field with a car, I was often the gofer for the executives at FBI Headquarters. I was happy to run errands, pick up Mr. Hoover's brokerage statements, or perform any other task. I was a street agent, but I often dined and played golf with senior FBI executives. It was excellent job security while attending law school. After a few months at this background stuff, I was transferred to Squad S-2, the KGB, now FSB, squad at the FBI Washington D.C. Field Office.

Supreme Court Justice Douglas

When I first arrived at the Washington D.C. Field Office, I was assigned to the Applicant Squad. My area was Northern Virginia, an area that included Arlington, Alexandria, and Fairfax County. I spent several months knocking on doors and interviewing witnesses, as a part of conducting background checks on White House staff members.

Some mornings, after obtaining my bureau car from the garage, I might drive over to the Hot Shoppe at the Marriott Key Bridge Hotel or some other venue to get a cup of coffee or breakfast before starting out to cover my leads. One morning, as I sat down at the counter at the Hot Shoppe, I noticed this white-haired older gentleman to my right. His newspapers were scattered all over the counter. He was a bit gruff as he had to move them to clear a place for me. Sometime later he finished breakfast and departed. I asked the older gray-haired waitress, who had been there ever since there had been a Hot Shoppe, "Wasn't that Supreme Court Justice (William O.) Douglas?" I thought this because he looked familiar and had received a lot of publicity lately for marrying a young female law student from one of his classes. She replied, "Oh yes, that was Justice Douglas. He comes in here every morning for breakfast. He goes for young girls, but he likes old ladies' cooking."

An Average Garden Variety Spy Case

Our squad dealt with known Soviet KGB personnel in the Washington D.C. area, most of whom had cover as diplomats or news correspondents. Each squad member was tasked with tracking one or more Soviets, depending on the extent of their known activities. Those with highly active Soviets might have only one case as I did.

It was a classic beginning of a spy case. Viktor Kopytin was a KGB agent undercover as a correspondent with the Russian News Agency TASS. He was in a D.C. bar and overheard the conversation between two Americans. One worked for Senator Tom Dodd on the Space and Aeronautics Committee. The other individual was tasked with keeping up with related issues with a Department of Defense think tank. The think tank representative later became my double agent. After listening at the next table for a while, Kopytin introduced himself as a Soviet journalist. He asked if they would mind if he joined in the conversations about Multiple Re-Entry Vehicles (MERVs) and defense policy.

Later, as they were leaving, Kopytin asked for the think tank American's phone number. The American's grandfather, who was Jewish, had emigrated from Russia to the United States years earlier. Kopytin had been an exchange student in the United States and was smooth and sophisticated. Kopytin had reportedly obtained a master's degree from the Columbia School of Journalism, but other sources mention UCLA. He once bragged that some of his classmates were now important U.S. journalists such as Marvin Kalb and his brother—important contacts for him. The American and Kopytin developed a common bond based upon their ties to Russia. As his security clearance required, the American reported his contact with a Soviet to the FBI. I, as the Soviet's case agent, on the KGB Squad of the FBI's Washington Field Office, encouraged him to continue this relationship.

Initially, the Soviets were suspicious about this American source. He was an unlikely candidate to turn against the USA. He had a great life with every advantage, so what would be his motive? Kopytin told the source he wanted him to meet several of his associates. That ended up with him going to a motel where Kopytin and a few other Soviets waited. We took photos of him entering the motel room with a Russian standing in the doorway.

When they inquired why he would help the USSR, as scripted he told them that while he probably would not feel comfortable living in Russia, he thought the bigger threat to world peace was the USA. He told them we were investing too heavily in the military and felt very emboldened, citing the USA handling of the Cuban missile crisis, etc. This apparently convinced the Soviets, and they bought into him.

There were three principal areas Kopytin was interested in having the source gather information. First, the Soviets were disturbed over deepening ties between China and America; second, they were concerned about our arms control policy, and they were troubled by American policy regarding USSR meddling in certain hotspots. At that time, the Middle East in the aftermath of the 1967 War was the most pressing. Later in the operation, when the source was deciding to leave Washington, Kopytin started urging him to stay and seek a position in the State Department or White House, where he would be exposed to international political issues. With hindsight, this would have helped to earlier confirm the existence of a foreign political directorate in the KGB that surfaced later in the Strategic Arms Limitation Talks (SALT).

Over subsequent weeks, Kopytin would ask the source for help and information on various unclassified matters. At about the same time, what turned out to be a double-agent case was getting started. Senator J. William Fulbright, a Democratic Senator from Arkansas (known in the intelligence community as Senator Half Bright) was seeking to embarrass the Nixon Administration and score points with the left. He chose to violate several laws by releasing to the public an extensive list of classified research studies being funded by the Department of Defense. The studies included those by defense contractors such as Rand Corporation, Battelle, and other such organizations. Most of these studies were classified Secret and above. These became a shopping list for Soviet spies to test the legitimacy of their sources. For example, if one worked for a government contractor, then they should have access to, or to be able to provide, the study.

Kopytin began asking my double agent source for certain classified studies, most of which were only provided after appropriate clearances. A special board connected with the National Security Advisor at the White House would authorize release. I recall once going to International Security Affairs at the Pentagon to discuss the release of a classified study pertaining to the Peoples' Republic of China. I will always remember the response of an ISA Official. He said, "We would love for the Soviets to know what we know about the Chinese. Sell it to them!" At the same time, we were putting people in jail for selling classified information.

Over a couple of years, the source and Kopytin met about every six weeks at restaurants throughout D.C. and the suburban areas. Each time, the source would pass certain information and reports, and the Soviet would usually provide $5,000 to $6,000 in brand new U.S. $20-dollar bills. We often wondered how much cash Soviet spies left the Soviet Embassy with and how much was paid to their sources. It was common knowledge then that Soviets skimmed money from that which was intended for their sources. One Soviet called it the "coefficient of danger." We were never concerned about our source who was comfortable financially, plus his father had a seat on the New York Stock exchange.

During the operation, the source relocated to Massachusetts with his job but continued to return to D.C. for the spy meets. We always put him in the better hotels, including the Hilton at 16th and K or the Watergate Hotel, as a part of his cover. The operation was funded by Soviet money. We would pay the hotel bills with cash after recording the serial numbers of the bills we spent, and then turn the remaining funds over to the special agent in charge's secretary for further efforts to trace the origin.

At one meeting at a popular D.C. bistro with my source, Kopytin was unusually pushy. When it came time to order dinner, the Soviet asked for recommendations. My American source, who had quite a sense of humor, said, "I think you should have the red snapper."

On occasions, we would photograph the two together in case there was ever a need to prosecute the Soviet. He did not enjoy diplomatic immunity, but great deference was usually given to foreign news personnel by our government. (As an aside, he was a classic scofflaw. Once I pointed out his car, typically illegally parked, to a D.C. police officer. The officer impounded the vehicle and found twenty-five parking tickets inside. This resulted in an unfavorable article in the Washington Post.)

What we were really learning was the specific targets of interests to the Soviets, often discernable from the questions they asked. Kopytin used to punch his finger into my double agent's chest and demand, "We want to know what your president is thinking. We want to know what your president is thinking!"

It was common practice in the United State intelligence and law enforcement community for many years to deny the existence of the Mafia—until Joseph 'Joe' Valachi revealed to the FBI that he was a member of a secret criminal society, La Cosa Nostra. Likewise, there was no recognition of a political branch in the KGB. We were still focused on chasing spies who wanted missile secrets when the USSR had missiles as good as ours. This came to the forefront later with the SALT or Strategic Arms Limitation Talks.

Eventually, my double agent decided that he would talk to the White House about the FBI's lack of interest in our case. I spent until 2AM in his hotel room at the Capitol Hilton reminding him that there might possibly be repercussions, but I did not dissuade him. He was growing more frustrated with the information he was providing not being taken seriously by our leadership, as was I. He was well connected politically and was a friend and contact of Doug Bailey, a principal campaign consultant for Vice President Gerald Ford. Bailey was close to Ambassador Robert Ellsworth, who was then working in the Nixon White House. Bailey arranged a meeting between my source and Ambassador Ellsworth. Afterwards, Ellsworth called a car and sent him to FBI Headquarters, initially to talk to Director J. Edgar Hoover. Upon arrival he was told Assistant Director William Sullivan would be talking to him instead.

My insecure supervisor, who had gotten a call from FBI Assistant Director Sullivan's office, came running through the squad room shouting, "Do you know what your double agent is up to? He is headed to FBI Headquarters?" "Really?" I replied, silently delighted. I was happy to see some action that would draw attention to the work we were doing.

Sullivan oversaw all national security matters for the FBI. As it turns out, my double agent source and Assistant Director Sullivan, both bright guys, had a delightful visit. It was probably the first time the FBI assistant director had talked to a real double agent in contact with a Soviet KGB agent. For a while, little if anything changed at FBI headquarters with my case. Due to the upper level of both the White House and FBI Headquarters we were dealing with, I had little concern about any fall-out for me from this meeting. It was unusual, though, for an FBI informant to walk into the White House to report that the FBI was not taking a case seriously.

"Do not embarrass the Bureau."

Late in his tenure as FBI Director, Mr. Hoover began to grow inward and protective of his legacy. The cardinal rule was "Do not embarrass the Bureau," which meant Mr. Hoover. He was sensitive of contacts in the news media for fear of adverse articles. Before we could interview a person in the media about KGB agents whom they had contact with, it was required that a background investigation be conducted, and permission be obtained from FBI Headquarters. Thus, it became doubly difficult in dealing with news media spies, as many of their contacts were with news media personnel.

If one followed the arbitrary headquarters rules to the letter, it would shut down all interviews with press personnel as a practical matter. As luck would have it, I was friends with Alan Cromley, the head of the Washington Bureau of the Daily Oklahoman in D.C. and president of the National Press Club. We were both active in the Oklahoma State Society, something my supervisor in

Richmond, Hershel Caver, advised me to do if I ever got to D.C. Cromley knew personally nearly all news personnel in D.C.

If our technical coverage indicated that my KGB agent was having lunch with some American news media type, instead of doing a full field background check and taking a month, I would call Alan, tell him that my Soviet had lunch with Mr. X of the New York Times, for instance, whereupon he might suggest that I not contact that person because of his or her leftist or anti-FBI leanings. Other times, he might say, for example, "Hell, Mr. X is an old Marine veteran. Do you want to talk to him?" Ten minutes later I would have a call from Mr. X, who would provide a report about what was discussed and become another press contact. It would be okay if someone called us instead. I became the "go to guy" for agents with Soviet bloc newsmen spies.

Mike Hudabaugh replaced Cromley as Press Club president, and I enjoyed the same relationship with him. These contacts would come in handy after I left the FBI when certain FBI executives wanted to get their story out discreetly during the ABSCAM sting operation. I would set up lunches for us.

Equally vexing at the time was that Mr. Hoover also forbade contact with universities for the same fear of potential embarrassment. The morning after each spy meet, my source and I, along with other agents from the squad, would meet to debrief him. Preparing the letter-head memorandums (LHM) from such debriefings was time-consuming. I grew tired of taking notes and was concerned that I might be missing something. I would thereafter put the old Dictaphone machine with the pink belts in a briefcase and sneak it out of the FBI office to the University of Oklahoma's Washington, D.C. office conference room, an office my wife Nancy ran. I would give the source the microphone and tell him: "Instead of 'I' say 'source' and instead of the Russian's name, say 'subject.'" He would dictate thirty pages or longer memos about what the Soviet was interested in, which drove my supervisor nuts. He was not accustomed to such detailed LHMs. The stenographers in the steno pool would then transcribe the pink belts for me to edit. My supervisor at one point even assigned another agent on our squad to me to do my paperwork.

A few days after one such debriefing, I picked up my neighbor and friend Lieutenant Colonel Jim Nelson, USAF, at the Pentagon to drive him to a place near Andrews AFB, where he could get a Kirby vacuum cleaner wholesale through one of my contacts. Jim's mother owned the tow truck service the Oklahoma City Police Department (OCPD) used back when I was on the OCPD. His brother Paul was my friend and the Administrator of the Tinker AFB Hospital who rushed through my FBI physical exam in 1961.

I knew Jim was working in the subject area that the Kopytin was talking about. I handed him a copy of the classified Secret memo from the recent spy meeting and suggested he read it as I drove. That evening he came over to my house and told me that he had had an uncomfortable afternoon. He said he was working with eight other people in the Pentagon on the U.S. position for the Strategic Arms Limitation Talks (SALT). From my secret memo it was clear to him that the Department of Defense (DOD) staff working on our SALT talks "position" were "not even in the right ballpark." He wanted to know how he could get an official copy.

The next morning, I went in to see my supervisor and told him of LTC Nelson's request. To my surprise, he told me to take the LTC a copy. When I got to the Pentagon, I was met by Jim Nelson. He ushered me into the office of a three-star vice admiral, who was deputy chief of the Joint Chiefs of Staff and the official in charge of SALT talks at DOD. Lowly LTC Nelson and lowly GS-12 FBI Agent George sat patiently in front of the Admiral's desk as he read the debriefing memo. Periodically his bushy gray eyebrows would twitch, and he would exclaim "those dirty bastards" as he turned the pages. When he finished reading, he asked a few questions about the background and bona fides of my source, and then said, "May I communicate with your headquarters?" My response was, "Certainly." What I did not know until 40 years later was that LTC Nelson and the admiral could tell from the Soviet's questions that our U.S. position in Geneva had been leaked, and the Soviet had it in chronological order.

The admiral immediately went to Secretary of Defense Melvin Laird, who called the Secretary of State, who called in the State Department FBI liaison and reamed him out. He demanded to know how many other operations like this were going on that they had not been informed about.

My case was one of the hottest in the Bureau for a brief time until the Soviets invaded Czechoslovakia and the disarmament talks were put off to the United States' advantage, so our side could regroup. In 1969, a Washington Post correspondent was kicked out of Moscow, and our TASS correspondent KGB chap was declared persona non grata—partly in retaliation, and partly to get rid of him. (According to Internet sources, Kopytin was later kicked out of Italy in 1984 for spying.) Kopytin's departure occurred during my last month of night law school at American University, where I was carrying 14 hours trying to finish there. It was a hectic time for me, and the paperwork was intensive as we closed out the case and finished that project.

Right Spy, Wrong Plane

We were periodically saddled with surveillance on one another's spies. On one such occasion we were directed to shadow a known KGB agent of Lithuanian extraction assigned to the Soviet Embassy in D.C. Alexi Zencavages was small in stature compared to most of the other diplomats. This chap had gotten the required permission from the State Department to travel to New York City. His case agent wanted to know what Alexi was doing while in New York. Was he making a spy meet, or was he simply there on legitimate embassy business? Our job was to confirm that he got on a plane. Then the New York agents would pick up the surveillance upon the target's arrival in New York City. They would endeavor to determine what he might be doing while there. We reciprocated for the New York Office with respect to known or suspected KGB Agents assigned to the United Nations or the consulate in New York City when they visited D.C.

On this day we tailed him to National Airport (now Reagan National Airport). Once inside the terminal, he seemed to be taking his time in getting to the gate for the Eastern Airlines Shuttle. Three of my squad members and I were hoping to get this assignment out of the way promptly. It was payday Friday, and traditionally we went to the Flagship Restaurant for a seafood lunch. Thus, this slow Soviet was beginning to interfere with our lunch plans. We could see outside the terminal window that the shuttle was already boarding.

I was dressed in a dark "Hoover Blue" suit, which was like those worn by Eastern Airlines employees at the time. I approached the Soviet and said "Sir, your plane is leaving," whereupon he picked up the pace toward the departure gate. This was back in the days when the steps folded down from the inside of the airplane. By the time we arrived at the gate, the steps were already being retracted. The aircraft had completed boarding. I approached the airline gate agent, identified myself by flashing my credentials, and told her to put the guy whom I pointed out to her on the plane.

The agent called the pilot and hustled the little spy out onto the tarmac as the pilot put the steps back down. I remember how forlorn and pathetic he appeared as he stood there alone on the tarmac with his briefcase, awaiting the descending steps with a hundred sets of eyes watching and wondering who this dignitary was who was holding up their flight. In any event, we finally got our ward on the plane, called the New York office, told them to look for him on the next shuttle, and went to lunch.

A few months later, while on a personal trip to New York City, I learned that the shuttle that departed on the hour went to La Guardia, and the shuttle that departed on the half hour went to Newark, New Jersey. We had put the little spy on the shuttle to New Jersey. It became clear why the New York agents had missed him upon arrival, as well as how close we came to creating an "international incident."

A Flat Tire

One of our tasks was to put selected Americans in touch with Soviet KGB Agents to develop a relationship and a double-agent situation. In one case, we had the Air Force Office of Special Investigations (OSI) identify an Air Force enlisted man of Lithuanian extraction.

We arranged for the airman to be in the parking lot of the Soviet's apartment complex when the Soviet arrived home in the evening. The Air Force person was pretending to deal with a flat tire. As the Soviet walked by the car, our Lithuanian Air Force enlisted man was loudly cursing in the Lithuanian language and lamenting his difficulty with changing a tire. This attracted the attention of the target. He engaged the enlisted man in a conversation in Lithuanian, subsequently developing a relationship. Once they established a relationship, the OSI, working with the CIA, would transfer the airman to an overseas military base (Korea, Egypt, etc.) to see who would come out of the woodwork to contact him. I do not know the rest of the story here, just the beginning, but this was one of the creative methods used at the time to confirm the identities of KGB personnel operating in other countries.

The Installation

The Soviet news agency correspondent Kopytin had been an exchange student at the University of California and appeared more American than many Americans. He was quite a ladies' man, though married to a beautiful Russian woman.

One of my sources was a young woman librarian

with an international organization. She had met Kopytin through a newsman friend while attending a correspondent's dinner. They struck up a relationship. Never underestimate a librarian. They are smart, well-read, patriotic, and some are even willing to work undercover, if necessary, to further the cause of freedom and democracy. Kopytin's method of operation was to call every month or so, tell her he was in the area, and ask if he could come by.

She lived in an efficiency apartment in Southwest DC near 4th and Eye Street on the sixth floor. By coincidence, my late wife, Nancy, whom I married in 1966, and I lived in the same development in another apartment building on the sixth floor. Her balcony was about two hundred feet away from our balcony. Our plan was to obtain some compromising photos that we might use against him. At the time, our perception was that his wife was probably jealous. We were in the middle of the Cold War and looking for opportunities to cause KGB officers difficulty.

With the librarian's permission, a fellow squad member and I installed a camera inside a large plastic clothes bag in her closet. We cut a hole through the drywall and mounted a two-way mirror, which faced the sofa-bed in the one room apartment. The FBI lab had fitted the camera with a receiver that would click the shutter whenever the microphone of a two-way radio was keyed. (Technology was not particularly good back then with low budget operations.) The limiting factor was that the two-way radio had to be no more than about two hundred feet away, and with no obstructions that might weaken the signal. We had sixty frames of film in the camera. The plan was to key the mic about every minute, thereby getting an hour of activity.

This matter dragged on for several weeks until one night the Soviet finally called again. Madame librarian tried to reach me on my beeper. Unfortunately, I was out at a law school class, and my beeper, which I had carried religiously for the past six weeks, had inadvertently been turned off. She then called my apartment and told my new bride that she was unable to reach me. She reported that Kopytin was on his way, and time was short. My wife had emergency instructions, so she turned on the two-way radio. The temperature outside was in the teens on the balcony. She was trying to dry her hair with one of those old backpack dryers with a bonnet on it and was dressed in a robe out in the bitter cold, while at the same time trying to take remote photos of a Soviet in bed. Her microphone clicks out in the cold became more frequent than one minute apart.

We thereafter pulled out the installation and Bob and I refinished the drywall in her apartment. A few months later, I was sitting in the back row at an in-service course down at Quantico when two guys from the FBI Lab came in. They had a big poster display of our camera setup and talked about the great installation we recently used in southwest D.C. I was the only one in the room who knew that, after all that effort, the only thing we got was an album of photos of a Soviet mixing himself in a drink and that the photos we did get were taken by my new bride. Mr. Hoover might have had us all on the next bus to Butte or worse had he known.

As an aside, the librarian enjoyed the attention of the several FBI agents she met those several months. On one occasion, around midnight, I was awakened by a phone call with the message, "Look out your balcony." I grabbed the binoculars and saw two of my squad members and the librarian waving their arms at me from her balcony. I had to get dressed, retrieve them from her apartment, and drive them home in northern Virginia in a snowstorm. The buses were no longer running that late. It turns out that they had taken her to a nearby bar and restaurant for dinner. Each had more than enough to drink.

Thirty years later I would learn from a former KGB officer, Oleg Kalugin, that both the Soviet correspondent and his wife were having affairs within the Soviet Embassy community, and that our efforts would have had no impact.

A few months later, after Kopytin was kicked out of the country, I had passed the Virginia bar exam and was hired as a GS-15 by the banking agency at the U.S. Department of Agriculture (USDA). My source was subsequently contacted by another Soviet, who directed him to meet the first Soviet who had been expelled from the U.S. , in Montreal, Canada. The source initially could not get the attention of anyone at the FBI, as the case was presumed concluded and closed. Here I was, putting together a spy meet in Canada from the USDA with the Royal Canadian Mounted Police (RCMP).

Thirty years later I would learn from KGB Major General Oleg Kalugin (who later got crossways with the KGB himself and was granted asylum in the U.S.) that Kopytin once planted a microphone in the Senate Armed Services Committee hearing room. The man got busy.

Spies I Have Known

At a going away party in 1994 for Senator David Boren, who was leaving the Senate to be the president of the University of Oklahoma, I spotted Oleg Kalugin in the crowd. I walked up beside him and asked, "Whatever happened to Viktor Kopytin?" Kalugin turned around and said, "Oh you know Viktor?" Then he mentioned that Viktor had gotten in some undisclosed trouble, but his wife had connections, and nothing happened to him.

A few months later, the Smithsonian Institution in Washington was running a weekly series on the Cold War titled "The Hammer and the Sickle." During the several weeks this series ran there were a string of presenters, mostly retired CIA Officers, or other Intelligence types. One week Kalugin was on the program as the presenter. I attended the event, and after Kalugin had finished his presentation, I approached him. I told him that I would like to get him together with some of the guys from the FBI Washington Field Office for lunch. He said that he would love to do that, and within a week or so he met me and Robert Feuer for lunch at the City Club. Feuer had been Kalugin's case officer, as I had been for Kopytin. We had an enjoyable two-hour lunch, bouncing stories back and forth of opposite sides of the intelligence business from 30 years earlier.

Kalugin told us one story of wanting to tour the United States during his summer vacation. Normally, the Soviets went back to Russia for a couple of weeks. He instead went to all the trouble to get State Department permission and all the approvals from his own government to drive to Florida. He and his wife drove south down Interstate 95—being followed, of course, by FBI agents. At one point his car broke down just before they arrived at their hotel. The FBI agents picked him and his wife up and drove them to the hotel.

The next morning, when he came out, his car, an old green Volkswagen, was repaired and ready to go. We got a laugh out of that. What he probably did not understand was that the FBI agents in North Carolina or South Carolina, wherever this happened, just wanted to get him out of their territory and get him into the next field office's area so they could go home to dinner or go on about their business. He said that he considered writing Mr. Hoover a thank you letter but figured that he would get all the agents in trouble, which was probably correct at the time.

Kalugin had overseen one of the most damaging spy cases at the time, known as the "Walker Spy Case." A former naval enlistee provided Kalugin with secret technology with respect to silent propellers for our nuclear submarines. U.S. technology was such at the time that the propellers were quiet and undetectable.

I had left the FBI by then, but the FBI's perception at that time was that Kalugin was leaving the country because he was in trouble. Instead, he was going back to the Soviet Union to be promoted to Major General in the KGB for his efforts in that spy case.

My fellow former agent, Robert Feuer, had been on what was known as the "Smile Program." This program consisted of selected agents who might approach Soviets from time to time and greet them with a big smile or say, "good morning," or at least be outside their apartment in the morning they were leaving for work. The hope was to develop a relationship and eventually to develop them into sources or get them to defect. Feuer had Kalugin as one of his "Smile" targets at an earlier time. Bob Feuer and a team of FBI agents followed Kalugin and his family from Washington DC to New York City, where they were to depart for the Soviet Union.

Kalugin and his family stopped at Howard Johnson's on the New Jersey Turnpike. He was in line to get a cup of coffee at the carryout. Bob Feuer walked up behind him and said, "Oleg Danilovich, (or whatever his middle name was), you don't have to go back." Kalugin turned around and said, "Oh. We are in the same business." That was the first indication ever that a Soviet might admit to spying activities. The approach, of course, did not work, and Kalugin went back to the Soviet Union. He was assigned to St. Petersburg with the KGB. After living in the United States for 30 years, he began to enforce Russia's laws as we would in the US. He promptly got himself crossways with the KGB for locking up the wrong criminals, and that got him kicked out of the organization.

He then ran for the DUMA, the Soviet Legislature, and was elected for a brief time. He told us how he had written Mikhail Gorbachev a six-page letter, when Mikhail became the head of the Soviet Union, telling him that if he did not get control of the KGB, the KGB would get control of him. Later, when the KGB was after Kalugin. a Russian Orthodox priest alerted him and concealed him from the KGB.

As an aside, Bob Feuer had retired, and he and his wife stopped for lunch at the same Howard Johnsons on the New Jersey Turnpike where he had sought to turn Kalugin several years earlier. A guy in the next booth was speaking Russian to his family, and they stuck up a conversation in English. The Russian speaker turned out to be the Russian Orthodox Priest who had hidden Kalugin when he was on the run from the KGB.

Eventually, Kalugin was granted asylum in the United States. He became a capitalist and was in a consulting business partnership with a former staffer from the Senate Intelligence Committee. He was involved in the "Spy Museum" in D.C. Kalugin used to send me Christmas cards. My wife and I were invited to his house for dinner one time in Bethesda, Maryland. The party guests consisted mostly of retired CIA or former intelligence types.

In 2008, one of my friends in Albuquerque, a retired FBI agent then with counterintelligence at the Sandia Labs, had occasion to go to Washington for a training program. One of the presenters at that program turned out to be former KGB Major General Oleg Kalugin. Kalugin began his presentation by mentioning that he had known a couple guys from the FBI's Washington DC Field Office. One of them was Bob Feuer, and he could not remember the other guy's name. He then popped a slide onto the screen, which consisted of a photograph of him, Bob Feuer, and me, taken at the City Club where we had had lunch back in the early nineties. I had provided him with a copy of the photo back then—one that was placed in the Grapevine, the monthly magazine from the Society of Former FBI Agents.

Spies Among Us

In Lynchburg, while I was assigned there, we had a college professor suspected of being a deep cover Soviet agent. There were both wiretaps and microphones located in the quarters of this individual and his wife. FBI Agents from the Washington D.C. field office came down frequently to monitor coverage and sometimes interview the professor. As the only FBI agent in Lynchburg most of the time, I got to meet several of the old-time spy catchers such as Pete Brent and Dudley Paine who came down from the Washington, D.C field office. I was never briefed on specifics concerning this professor, as this matter was separate from my responsibility as the resident FBI agent.

I remain a fan of FBI Director J. Edgar and the organization he built. The opportunity to serve in Hoover's FBI was one of my big breaks in life. It opened doors and opportunities to me as a farm boy from Oklahoma who would never have dreamed these existed. He was an old Victorian gentleman who probably should have retired after catching the Nazi spies in World War II, but no one pissed on him when he was alive.

Society of Former FBI Agents

When I left the FBI in October of 1969 after eight years and five transfers, it was unthinkable not to join the ex-agents' group, the Society of Former Special Agents of the Federal Bureau of Investigation. During most of the time I was in private law practice in Washington, D.C., I served on the Legal Affairs Committee. I was the one nearest the office at Quantico and handled the day-to-day legal questions and problems. I once saved them a bundle in mailing costs by getting a favorable ruling from the Post Office Department based on their non-profit status. In later years, I served as the chair of the Recruitment Committee.

I occasionally attended the Washington, D.C. Chapter lunches but did not have a lot in common with many of the people. Many were formerly from the FBI Headquarters, and some tended to drink their lunch. I was in a busy law practice and did not have much time for that.

It was shortly after we relocated to New Mexico in 2002, that my wife, Nancy, was diagnosed with a terminal illness. As luck would have it, my support system were the old fellows that I had worked with forty years earlier as FBI agents, as opposed to the partners in two different 200-lawyer law firms. I started attending regular chapter meetings and learned that five of the eight guys who served in the Atlantic City resident agency with me in the sixties had lost spouses to cancer. I heard from them on a frequent basis during my wife's illness, which meant a lot. Shortly after Nancy's death, I was watching Fox News and saw Gary Aldrich, a former FBI agent, on television defending the FBI on some policy issue opposite some chap with the Clinton administration. The light bulb came on for me. I remembered that he was an agent who had applied and had been blackballed or rejected. I had known the people involved in that costly mistake. I did not have much else to do at the time and was ticked off at the world. I wrote the then president of the Society and suggested that Aldrich was doing what the society should be doing, defending the FBI on TV, and that he should have his membership. I noted that his wife, also a former agent, was a current member.

Gary Aldrich had been an FBI Agent posted in the Clinton White House. He authored a tell-all book about some of the things that went on there. His source for his book material had been Linda Tripp of Clinton and Monica Lewinsky scandal fame. I had served as the trustee for Linda Tripp's legal defense fund at certain points. I had mentioned Gary's name once to George Saunders, also a retired FBI agent, who had worked at the White House for many years. When I mentioned Aldrich's name, he uncharacteristically went crazy. So, I knew there was some bad blood there and that he was behind Gary being rejected.

The Society President, Tom Tierney, blew me off, so I wrote him another letter. When I delved into the matter, I learned that Ed Fleck, a former agent in Tampa, Florida, had tried to fix the Aldrich mess and had been rebuffed at every turn. He got together the required one hundred members signatures necessary to fix this problem, so they then changed the bylaws to require two hundred signatures for such changes. I teamed up with him and, using the chat room called XGBOYS, started posting messages about Gary Aldrich, titled "Promote Gary from the Spouse's Program." Sean McWeeney, a former FBI official and society official, posted a message to the effect, "How dare you trash the leadership?" That was because I was the first one who had ever questioned any of their stupid decisions. I also heard from Charles George, a lawyer in Florida and a former president of the society, accusing me of being Gary Aldrich's lawyer. At that point I had not even met Aldrich.

Over a relatively brief period, Ed Fleck and I put together 250 personal member endorsements and attached them to Gary's application and re-submitted it. The hardest part was to get Gary to re-apply. His attitude was, "Screw me once, it's your fault; screw me twice, it's mine." He thought the board should fix it on their own. Eventually, I said to Gary, "Do you just want the issue, or do you want to be a member?" He allowed us to go ahead and submit the papers.

It should have been handled in about two days under the circumstances, particularly considering that the society had been losing members for a few years—some of it over the Aldrich matter. They still sat on the application for five months to show us how arrogant and out of touch they were. The Aldrich problem stemmed from one member who resented Aldrich once being offered a job at the White House that the detractor held.

Throughout this project I made a lot of friends, made a few enemies, and re-established contact with many of the people that I had worked with during my eight years and five transfers as an FBI agent. As soon as Gary got his membership card, Ed and I began to hear from others who had been blackballed, to the effect of, "I got screwed also. Please fix mine." We successfully un-blackballed over a dozen former FBI agents, most of whom had been rejected because someone did not like them. One even broke down in tears when I told him his membership card was on the way. Being a member counted for much, especially for marketing their private investigation businesses.

In the process, we also changed the bylaws to more easily qualify for having "serve[d] with due fidelity to their Oath of Office"—which is now about anything short of a felony conviction. A new President was elected, Jerry Emmons, whom I had not known very long. Jerry, over my protest, appointed me chair of the Recruitment and Retention Committee. I argued strongly that Membership and Recruitment should not be separate committees, as they handled essentially the same function. We did not need one group trying to keep people out and another group trying to get people in.

After having restored several "blackball-ees" to membership, I urged the then Membership Committee head, Bill Herndon, to go through all the files of those who had been rejected over the years and to give me a list of those who met the current standard of service with due fidelity to their Oath of Office and not a convicted felon. He provided a list of a dozen who fit that category. We set about locating and contacting them. Some were no longer living. Some were understandably hostile at first.

For example, before this list, it had come to my attention that Danny Coulson, who was head of the Hostage Rescue Team for the FBI, had been rejected. I had surreptitiously gotten access to correspondence that indicated a group in Oregon and some of the board members were going to screw him if he ever applied. I was not aware that he had ever applied and been rejected until I asked the executive director, Scott Erskine, one day, and he indicated he had in fact applied and had been turned down.

I set about to locate Coulson—who, as it turned out, was then head of security for PGA Tours and is seen on FOX news occasionally opining on anything FBI related. I called my friend and former roommate Bill Carter in Oklahoma City, whom I knew used to be in Coulson's carpool. He did not know where Coulson now lived but said that Buck Revell, the former number two guy in the FBI, would know. I happened to have known Revell for many years, so I called him and told him why I was trying to reach Danny Colson. His reply was, "I never understood that crap; that ought to be fixed."

Fifteen minutes later I got a call from Danny Colson, who had been directed to call me by Buck Revell. He was hostile. He said, "I was urged to apply by friends. I got blackballed and embarrassed, and I don't want any part of you all." So, for the next year I would pepper him with messages and information on the change in the bylaws and all that sort of thing. After about a year of that, I got Buck Revell and several of his friends to call him, along with me, all on one day, telling him to get his application in so we can make the next publication date of The Grapevine—our monthly magazine, which publishes lists of applicants and members. He did, and now he is a member. Periodically I see him on Fox News, where he is a frequent contributor, and I sometimes send him a message congratulating him on his presentation. I will usually get some humorous reply from him, saying, "Oh, I just made it up."

Another name on that list of twelve rejected ex-agents was Joe Jackson, who had been the special agent—of all places—in charge in Jackson, Mississippi. As I got into the details, he had been running the Detroit office, as the assistant agent in charge. The special agent in charge, Ken Walton, had been transferred back to headquarters from Detroit. Jackson had a situation in one of the resident agencies where the agents could not get along with one another, so he transferred a couple of them to headquarters. Jackson eventually retired and applied to the society. These agents resented being transferred and were able to get him rejected under the prior system.

I contacted Jackson, assured him that we had changed the rules and that there was no problem now. I urged him to apply, as did Jim Ingram, his chapter chairman. Ingram was prominent in the Civil Rights era with the Mississippi Civil Rights folks. He had also headed the New York and Chicago FBI offices. I had no inkling there was any problem until I was getting on a plane in Albuquerque to fly to Lake Tahoe for a regional meeting. I knew that his process had to go to the board because it had not been unanimous at the Membership Committee. I had also been assured by Emmons and Bernes, the past president and the president-elect, that there was no problem.

I got a call on my cell phone from Jackson, asking, "What's going on with the FBI Boys and Girls Club? One of your Board of Directors is trying to intimidate my references into withdrawing." When I arrived at Lake Tahoe, I found that Ed Armento, one of the board members, was bad mouthing Jackson to anyone who would listen to him. I was still assured that there was no problem.

I was waiting outside the boardroom to make my happy little presentation on the accomplishments of the Recruitment Committee when Rich Bernes came out and informed me that by a vote of nine to five, they had blackballed Jackson again. One of the board members did not like him. The then president, Andy Palumbo, avoided me for two days, until I finally cornered him and all he could mumble was, "But the chapter wanted him." I promptly pulled down the happy little recruitment committee message on the society website since everything that we had done had just been scuttled.

I proceeded to organize Jackson's friends. I had his mentor, former Assistant Director Ken Walton, weigh in, as did Jim Ingram, who made a trip to the next meeting in Orlando to make a presentation to the board. I had convinced Jackson to "appeal," something that was unprecedented. The upshot of it was that this time they voted nine to five the other way, in favor of Jackson. But not before I had received a FedEx envelope on my front doorstep with a one-line letter from Andy Palumbo saying, "Your services as Chairman of the Recruiting Committee are terminated immediately." These can be very petty little people. In any event, I still served as the secretary for the New Mexico Chapter for some time thereafter and wrote the monthly bulletin.

Nationwide Concealed Carry

After 911, Congress passed HR-218. This legislation was to allow nationwide concealed-carry of firearms for retired law enforcement officers who had 15 or more years of service. In 2007 the law was revised to drop the word "retired," and it lowered the law enforcement service period to ten years, provided one had a photo I.D. card from their old agency and qualified annually at a police department firing range. Since I had three years with the Oklahoma City Police Department and eight years with the Federal Bureau of Investigation, that totaled more than ten years. I asked the FBI to send me a photo ID Card. They did, 43 years after I had left. The original card indicated that I had retired in 1969. This would suggest that I was over one hundred years old. Later I was provided a new ID that reflected that I had separated in 1969. I take my Santa Fe former FBI agents to the Albuquerque Police Range for our annual firearms qualification. I could legally carry a concealed weapon in New York City if I chose, but that is the last thing I want to do after carrying one for 11 years.

USDA, Advance Man, and the Army

Law Schools—All Four of Them

I started at the Oklahoma City University evening law school in August of 1961. I was still on the Oklahoma City Police Department, having just graduated from Central State College, now the University of Central Oklahoma. I had noticed that the well-dressed guys driving the big cars were lawyers, my motivation. I thought, "Wow! I could make $500 a month doing divorce cases."

Some of the beginning law-school classmates were my fellow OCPD Officers Royce Hodges, my partner much of the time I was there, and Jack Thorne. Jack would later become a judge. Also with us was George DeHarde, then a clerk in the local FBI Office and later an FBI agent, and Jack Neilson, then the only Secret Service agent in Oklahoma.

Jack Nielson had earlier encouraged me to apply to the Secret Service. Several of us OCPD officers had earlier taken the Civil Service Treasury Law Enforcement Exam, which covered Alcohol, Tobacco, and Firearms, the Secret Service, Customs, and other agencies then in the Treasury Department. I never heard from the Treasury Department until later and chose to start law school.

The first night of law school, Dean John Hervey, who had earlier been dean at the University of Oklahoma Law School, gave a welcome speech to the beginning class. He went on about the diverse backgrounds of the new students and their academic achievements. Finally, he said, "We even have one student who has college credit in Bait and Fly Casting." It was my partner, the late Royce Dean Hodges, who had a physical education degree from Central State. Royce dropped out after the first semester and later went to ATF with several other OCPD officers. His brother Chock stayed for a career with OCPD.

Special Agent in Charge Earl Brown gave me my law school exams from the first semester at OCU in his office in Richmond, Virginia. I had to leave for the new FBI agents' class before finals. I was obsessed with wanting to finish a law degree, though, but there were no night law schools in Virginia at the time. When I was transferred to the Newark, New Jersey, FBI Field Office, I enrolled in Seaton Hall Law School. It was downtown in Newark near the FBI Office. Three weeks later, Special Agent in Charge (SAC) Ralph Bachman learned of this. He called me into his office and told me that the FBI had hired me without a law degree, and the only reason I was going to law school was to get another job and he was not going to cooperate with me. That was not necessarily my plan at the time. He summarily transferred me to the Atlantic City Resident Agency. In hindsight, he did me a favor, as I would have never survived trying to complete law school in a relatively small office such as Newark where all agents were called out when some major event happened.

A year later my opportunity to get back in law school arose when I was transferred to Washington, D.C. to work the background checks for White House staffers. Not knowing how long I would be in Washington, I took a chance and enrolled in Catholic University Law School (CU). At the time it was located at Connecticut and N Street not too far from the FBI office. After a year, the CU Law School moved to the main Catholic University campus, which was less convenient for me. After two years at CU, by luck, I happened to be on a flight with, and sat by, Dean John Hervey, who now accredited law schools for the American Bar Association. He had been Law School dean at both Oklahoma University and Oklahoma City University (OCU) law schools while I was there the one semester. He suggested I switch to American University, as it was giving the Juris Doctor (JD) degree at the time, while CU was still giving the LLB degree. He made phone calls, and I switched. My last semester, I carried fourteen hours while running a top double-agent case with the FBI. I took the Virginia Bar and passed, much to my surprise.

The USDA and Farmers Home Administration

By the summer of 1969 I had completed a law degree at the American University and had passed the Virginia Bar. I was still on the FBI's KGB Squad, though my Soviet had recently been kicked out of the country. I met a former Congressman from Oklahoma, James V. Smith, at a Capitol Hill cocktail party. He was impressed with me and wanted to hire me as his executive assistant. At the time he was the administrator of the Farmers Home Administration, the banking agency in the U.S. Department of Agriculture. He hired both me and Marshall Burkes in hindsight merely because we were from Oklahoma. Marshall was a PhD Economist from Purdue.

I went from a GS12 FBI agent in one day to a GS-15 the next day at the USDA, the Civil Service equivalent of a one-star general. This certainly impressed the hell out of the guys on the KGB squad. I also took my supervisor's secretary, Vermell Wheeler, with me to the agency. This was not to work with me. Vermell was the only Black squad secretary in the Washington Field Office (WFO) and was miserable at the FBI with her difficult supervisor. She later became the personnel officer for one of the USDA agencies in addition to having a career in the Army Reserve. Special Agent in Charge (SAC) at WFO Joseph Purvis, to each of our credit, told me when I left that I could always come back to the FBI (and I received an autographed photo of Mr. Hoover).

Smith had been a one-term Congressman from Oklahoma and had lost his next election. When the Nixon Administration came into office, he was able to obtain this appointment, which turned out to be a big mistake for the administration. He was a high school graduate and a lay preacher in the Church of Christ. He had never served in the military or any other large organization. The only people that ever worked for him were those folks who threw the bales of hay on the truck on his farm.

Smith, with no management experience, was placed in charge of an agency with 6,000 employees and a $3 billion annual budget. He set out to spend much of the budget in the State of Oklahoma to get re-elected to Congress. There were days when I would say, "Mr. Smith, you can't do this. You are going to go to jail. We are all going to go to jail with you." He would periodically say, "Come on, let's go down the hall and smoke out a Democrat." I had to tell him they were all Democrats.

I knew that this national agency was part of USDA that made loans directly to farmers or for housing in rural communities or cities under 10,000 population. I did not know that these were both short- & long-term loans (1 to 30 years) for operations, machinery, upgrades, and long-term purchases of land with a county office base through throughout the U.S. The only source of funds came from the annual Federal budget, so there was an immediate, continuing cash flow delay on the revolving of the loan funds back to Farmers Home, even when the loan was paid back in full.

Before a national election, it was tempting for the incumbent party to commit more loans than could be funded (honored) from next year's budget. That had happened again in 1968. Farmers Home was selling a few "insured notes" (Full Faith & Credit of U.S.) to individuals and a couple of union pension funds in New York City. My friend, Marshall Burkes, who lived in San Francisco, was selected to find a way to attract substantial and sustainable long-term funds. This was his project, but I participated in most of the meetings. This gave me the opportunity to meet most of the top Wall Street underwriters. Heady stuff.

Marshall's assignment created the need for what became the "Block Sale of Farmers Home Notes." Such a security investment required the collaboration of the Wall Street leadership, the USDA leadership, the US Treasury Department leadership, many attorneys and, of course, the necessary and specific approval of the Comptroller General. The purpose of this instrument was to sell Farmers Home insured notes in sizeable blocks of $1 million or more and to attract major national securities brokers with institutional investors. The objective was to sell an "asset" that was not considered a "borrowing" of funds. Several billion dollars were brought in over the next couple of years. Wall Street used this concept for national single-family home securities. This securitization of mortgages (with or without principal or interest payments) became the primary investment vehicle of the national housing industry as led by Wall Street for the next four decades, then quality standards were abused, leading to the financial crisis of 2008.

Alaska

Shortly into my stint with the USDA, a lobbyist for the U.S. Plywood Corporation got to Smith and convinced him that the Farmers Home Administration should finance a company town in the Tongass National Forest in Alaska in the name of "rural development." The company did not want to be stuck with a bunch of housing in the middle of nowhere if the Japanese stopped buying the plywood they planned to manufacture there. As things moved along, Mr. Smith and I were going to go to Alaska to look at this deal, though I was never a part of any meeting between Smith and the lobbyist.

The trip continued to evolve to the point where we were to take our wives. My wife Nancy was eight months pregnant, and here we were going to Alaska in February. Her doctors assured her it was okay if she was on a pressurized airplane. U.S. Plywood's Lockheed Jet Star with the company Vice President in tow picked up our party at Dulles Airport. We flew to Great Falls, Montana, where we refueled on our way to Juneau, Alaska. Unfortunately, Juneau airport was socked in. We were circling there above the clouds with Japanese and American airplanes. After a brief time at this, we were diverted to Sitka, the old Russian capital. It was a hairy landing, as the single runway jutted out in the middle of the bay with water on each side as we landed. We were then picked up by a Grumman Goose, an old pontoon plane. Our party flew to Juneau, just above the water and under the weather. The governor and his party were waiting for us at the airport.

My wife was sick as could be on our pontoon plane flying just above the water. She was getting a lot of attention from the Vice President. Things like that never sat well with Mr. Smith, who expected all the attention.

The Alaska Legislature was in session. They had to kick a few people out of the Baronoff Hotel, the only hotel in Juneau of any quality at the time, to make room for our party.

Smith promptly got on Alaskan television and told all the listeners how the U.S. government was going to finance $100 million worth of housing for this new company town. I started looking at the details of the deal, which heretofore had not been shared with me. I quickly determined that the Tongass National Forest was in the Borough of Juneau, or City of Juneau. Our statutory authority permitted us to loan money in rural areas or communities with a population of under 10,000. Again, I had to tell Mr. Smith he could not do it.

It was a quiet ride back to Washington. My office shortly thereafter became the men's room in the South Agriculture Building for several weeks. Of course, I got the blame. No one could control Smith. I was usually the buffer between him and the Assistant Secretary, Tom Cowden to whom he technically reported. They would not speak to one another. Dr. Cowden, former Dean of Agriculture from Michigan State, would tell me, "Peyton, you go tell Smith such and such." Smith would say, "Peyton, you go back and tell Dr. Cowden such and such." I was getting beat up on both ends as the messenger.

At the start of the second Nixon term, they had all the presidential appointees submit a letter of resignation as a show of loyalty. They kept Smith's. He never listened to any advice. I am confident that someone told the poor guy not to be welding on a combine in the middle of a wheat field in windy Oklahoma. He died in the fire that he had started.

I had left a good job, had a wife and new baby, and here I was in this mess. As luck would have it, and since I am one of the luckiest guys in the world, Dr. Cowden plucked me out of the Farmers Home Administration and put me on the Congressional Liaison Staff in the Office of the Secretary of Agriculture. There I worked directly with Secretary Clifford Hardín, former Chancellor of the University of Nebraska. He left shortly thereafter to head Ralston Purina and was replaced by Earl Butz, the greatest, nicest boss I ever had. Earl had been Dean of Agriculture at Purdue University. I went through the 1972 Presidential campaign as one of his advance men. He was a surrogate presidential candidate and an extremely popular speaker in the Farm Belt. Nixon was in China or focusing on it quite a bit that year and really did not campaign very much. He had left the campaigning to his cabinet members and other presidential appointees. Four of us advance men leap-frogged one another to event after event for a year. It was heady stuff, and campaigning could be fun. I could have an Air Force plane pick us up or one of many corporate aircraft. We set the pace for the other cabinet secretaries. The White House advance staff sent a memo to all the cabinet level departments telling them that this was the way to get it done. They provided one of my itineraries as an example when we blitzed several states in a couple of days.

Congressional Liaison

After the Alaska debacle, while I was in limbo with the Farmers Home Administration, the personnel director of the Agriculture Department, Sy Pranger, assigned me to run training programs called "Seminars in Executive Development," which I conducted in several places throughout the country, including Palo Alto, California, and places in Virginia. Sy had been the personnel director at Farmers Home. We would have senior executives from different agencies—Soil Conservation, Forest Service, Food and Nutrition, you name it—together for training a program. It was an effort to try to get the far-flung agency employees of the USDA to talk to one another.

Also, during this limbo period, I was the Secretary's representative on what was known as the Interagency Economic Development Committee. We representatives of various cabinet departments would fly out to the various locations where military bases were being closed or cut back and explain to them how our agencies were going to take up the slack left by losses from the Defense Department. We would travel to all the bright spots like Crane, Indiana, and McAlester, Oklahoma, and so on.

On one of these trips, we were flying over West Virginia headed toward Indiana on an Air Force Convair 880. I looked out my window and saw that the propeller on my side of the plane was not spinning. We made an emergency landing on some mountaintop airport. The Air Force sent another plane to pick us up and flew us on to our destination.

Once while on the Congressional Liaison staff, I was the Secretary's representative on a House agriculture field trip to California. Fowler West, Congressman Pogue's administrative assistant; Christine Gallagher, House Agriculture Committee staff director, and I were the only non-Congressional members on this trip. We toured agriculture facilities all over California and saw the various special crops and agriculture I had never seen the likes of. It was only toward the end of the trip that I realized what it was all about. We were in Fresno, California, for one stop. The itinerary indicated "barbecue at one of the river ranches." I noticed that Congressman Frank Denholm, also a former FBI agent, chose not to go to the event. (He was the one that asked a question at the hearing about the Nixon taping system in the White House.)

In any event, each of us so-called "visiting dignitaries" were picked up in a separate car, a late model luxury car, and a farmer was with each of us as a passenger. We drove several miles to a huge ranch gate. Deputy sheriffs were checking off names to assure that no riff raff got in. We drove a few more miles and came to one of the most beautiful settings I had ever seen. It was on the banks of the King River.

It turned out to be a sit-down dinner that would have put the old Jockey Club restaurant in D.C. at the time to shame. I was sitting at the head table as the Secretary of Agriculture's representative. Only then did I finally realize what this trip was all about. I lived in fear that I would be called on to make a few remarks and would end up in Jack Anderson's column the next day. It turns out that the owner of the ranch was Russ Giffin, who was getting $4 million a year for not growing cotton on his 99,000 acres of land. That is what this trip was all about, so Giffin could schmooze the House Agriculture committee so that he kept getting his $4 million a year in taxpayer subsidies. Fortunately, I did not get called upon to speak.

During my Congressional Liaison Staff time with the U.S. Department of Agriculture, officials of the U.S. government, and the South Korean government decided it would be a great idea to start a cattle operation in South Korea. I was sent as the Secretary's representative to a ceremony at Tinker Air Force Base, attended by the governor of Oklahoma and a Congressional delegation. We watched as they loaded about one hundred feeder calves onto an Air Force C-141 cargo plane. Again, though prepared, I did not have to deliver any remarks on behalf of the Secretary of Agriculture. We did produce a lot of jokes about the project, though, such as "The Herd Shot Round the World" or "Operation Bull Shipper."

Advance Man

Darvid Quist, John Foltz, Roger Knapp and I were the crack advance team for the Secretary. My first visit to New Mexico was while serving as Secretary of Agriculture Butz's advance man. We were campaigning for the re-election of President Nixon and the election of Albuquerque City Councilman Pete Domenici to the U.S. Senate. I had gone to New Mexico to advance a trip by the secretary designed to shore up support in the southeast region of the state. One dusty Sunday afternoon, I flew to Clovis, New Mexico, with one of Domenici's aides who had an airplane. We drove around the town trying to scope out the best place for events. We learned that the cattle auction was on the day of the week of our appearance, and farmers would be there for "sale day." We wanted to do some sort of rally, preferably at the high school. We drove around Clovis High School that dusty Sunday afternoon and came to a band room. Parked in front was a Volkswagen literally plastered with "Re-elect Nixon" stickers. This was a surprise because the area was heavily Democratic.

We walked in an open door to the band room and struck up a conversation with the VW owner. He turned out to be the Band Director of the pride of Clovis, its 111-piece marching band. The band, under his direction, had won about every award offered in their part of the country. Seizing the opportunity, I suggested to the band leader that perhaps we could have a rally at Clovis High School. The band could play for Secretary Butz and Senate candidate Domenici. The secretary would then tell President Nixon, and we might be able to get his band included in the inaugural parade. This was about the only honor or recognition that the band had not received.

This person turned out to be right out of the show "The Music Man." Even though a Republican in a strongly Democratic area, he was one of the most respected by people in Clovis. I went on to Amarillo, where I met up with the secretary, who was there for another event. We returned the next day on the Air Force Jet. We did our thing with the Secretary and the Senate candidate at the cattle auction. I had both men patting the cows in the sale ring and talking to farmers there. There were plenty of cameras and photo ops.

We then moved by motorcade over to the Clovis High School Gymnasium. Through the efforts of the band leader, they had closed schools in the entire county and bussed in students, parents, and teachers for this big rally. Secretary Butz gave a super-inspirational speech, closing with the last four letters of the word American, "I Can." Domenici did his thing, followed by the Clovis Highschool's marching band opening inside the gymnasium with a deafening roar. Their repertoire, designed for Indianan Earl Butz, included the songs "Back Home in Indiana," "Wabash Cannonball," and any other song they thought he might like. This visit was the super success we had hoped for. We blitzed all the newspapers in that part of New Mexico with Secretary Butz and candidate Pete Dominici's photographs on the front page. There were lengthy articles and considerable TV coverage. My mission was to make the six and ten o'clock news and be above the fold in all the newspapers. I went on to the next location and thought nothing more about it until, as Paul Harvey would say, "and now for the rest of the story."

Some three months later, in early January 1973, I was sitting in my Congressional liaison staff office at USDA when I received a call from someone at the Republican National Committee. His first words upon my answering were, "George, did you promise some guy in Clovis, New Mexico, his band could be in the inaugural parade?" I replied, "Hell yes. They did a fantastic job." The rub had arisen because President Nixon, on his final trip to California before the election, had stopped off in Albuquerque for a big rally featuring the Albuquerque High School Band. As far as I know, we were responsible for New Mexico having two bands in the inaugural parade that year. I was telling this story to Senator Domenici over dinner with his wife and mine in D.C. in 2000. He said he knew it was one hell of a mess but did not know who had caused it.

Every Minute A Capsule of Energy

Secretary Butz was 63 years old at the time. We thought he was ancient. Mrs. Butz used to yell at us, claiming we were going to kill him. The truth of the matter was that he was killing his advance men, all of whom were in their thirties. In addition to being a sought-after speaker, he was a most remarkable guy in that I could say, "Mr. Secretary, you have 20 minutes." He could fall asleep, sleep twenty minutes, and awake perfectly refreshed. A few times a week his routine was to leave his office around 4PM in the limo to Andrews Air Force Base. There he might board an Air Force C-140, the Lockheed Jet Star, and for example, fly to Baton Rouge, Louisiana. He might deliver a keynote speech at the Farm Bureau Convention, attend a fundraiser and a fat cat reception, and then be wheels up at 9PM back to Washington, D.C.

Most people did not know that once he got on the plane at Andrews, he might sleep on the sofa for much of the three-hour flight to Baton Rouge. At 9PM, after boarding the plane back to Washington, he might sleep another two hours. Then he wondered where we were at 7AM the next morning when he would be in the office. I might ride back to D.C. with him, but often it was only to prepare for the next event where I might catch up with him again in a few days. We advance men leapfrogged one another across the farm belt.

I had a letter in my pocket signed by former Attorney General John Mitchell, head of the Committee to Re-elect the President. The letter gave me the authority to cancel any event that did not meet our requirements. We were sometimes ruthless in redoing schedules. The locals might cram the schedule for their own purposes with local dignitaries and entertainers. If we left it to them, our guy might not get on the podium until 10PM. The White House advance staff preached that every minute was a capsule of energy for our dignitary, and we did not want to waste a minute. We would time how long it took the elevator to get to the fifth floor, or wherever we were going, with a stopwatch. Likewise, we timed how long it took to get from the airport with a police escort to the downtown event. We were aware that the propeller airplanes of that day had to take ten or fifteen minutes revving up their engines to increase their manifold pressure before taking off. Jets could take off right away. On the propeller planes, I would direct that the pilots have the plane running when we got there, only shutting down the engine on the stair step side. Once we got on board, they would start up that engine, and we would quickly be back in the sky.

This was before today's campaign restrictions. I could pick up the phone and have a corporate plane pick us up in the middle of the night in one place and another corporate aircraft pick us up to go on to our next stop for political or campaign events. We also had the Air Force's Special Air Missions at our disposal for official events. They would provide C-140s, Lockheed Jet Stars, for long flights and twin-engine Cessnas, or the like, for short ones.

A few of the many events I played a role in throughout 1972 are listed below:

<u>Charleston, South Carolina.</u> There the Secretary spoke to 1100 people at the South Carolina Republi-

can Convention, and I took him to meet General Mark Clark of World War II and the Korean War fame who lived in the Francis Marion Hotel.

Baton Rouge, Louisiana. We attended the Louisiana Farm Bureau Convention.

Houston, Texas. We went to the Shamrock Hilton Hotel for the 95th annual convention of the Texas and Southwestern Cattle Raisers Association. Ranching is a big business in Texas.

Atlanta, Georgia. We attended the 19th National Republican Women's Conference in honor of Mrs. Richard Nixon.

Trenton, New Jersey. We went here to meet with the New Jersey Agriculture Society.

Harrisburg, Pennsylvania. Secretary Butz spoke at the Council of Farmers' dinner attended by about three hundred Pennsylvania legislators and agriculture officials.

Boone, North Carolina. This was for the annual meeting of the 5,000 members of the Blue Ridge Electric Coop.

Jackson, Mississippi. We attended a meeting of the Catfish Farmers of America at the Jackson Coliseum followed by a catfish luncheon for 5,000 attendees.

Baton Rouge, Louisiana. Secretary Butz was the keynote speaker at a banquet of the Louisiana Farm Bureau Federation.

Lubbock, Texas. Here we boarded Senator Tower's Beechcraft Queen Air in Dallas and flew to Lubbock, where the Secretary spoke to about five hundred persons at the convention center in honor of Senator Tower.

Galesburg and De Kalb, Illinois. We attended a Farm Progress show in Galesburg with Congressman Les Ahrens and then went to DeKalb for a pork barbeque at

Kishwaukee College and another speech.

Dallas, Texas. The Secretary was keynote speaker at the American Banker Convention.

Kansas City, Missouri. We visited the Future Farmers of America Convention attended by 11,000 members.

Tulsa, Oklahoma. The Secretary was the keynote speaker for Congressman Page Belcher appreciation and retirement dinner.

Galveston, Texas. We attended the state's Republican Convention. That same day Secretary Butz and Senator John Tower participated in loading the tanker S.S. Manhattan with grain for Bangladesh. One of the high points was meeting Captain Ernest D. Kachikis, the Captain of the S.S. Manhattan. He took us on board and gave us a tour of his huge ship. I never understood how they got that oil tanker cleaned up enough to put wheat in it, but they did.

Cincinnati, Ohio, and Springfield, Illinois. The Secretary was the keynote speaker for the Soybean Association Convention in Cincinnati. From there we had to pick up Mrs. Butz in Indiana for our trip to Springfield. I had her waiting in a car at the end of the runway. We were not coming to the terminal due to time pressures. Our Air Force jet touched down, taxied to the end of the runway, and spun around. The steps were lowered, she boarded, and we were back in the air in about a minute enroute to Springfield. Secretary Butz was met by Illinois Governor Ogilvie and other Illinois dignitaries for a tour of the Illinois State Fair. I had Secretary Butz and Governor Ogilvie milking a cow with the TV cameras rolling. We had a press conference on the grounds and greeted some of the winners from the state fair exhibitors. We toured the facility on a golf cart. Secretary Butz then addressed 5,000 people assembled for an auction. At one point during the tour of the fairgrounds, I had Secretary Butz on the stage with the cast of the then popular Nashville television program "Hee-Haw." Junior Samples acted as a straight man for the Secretary along with Grandpa Jones.

St. Croix, U.S. Virgin Islands, and Freeport, Bahamas. These locations were a payoff for the grueling pace of the campaign for me and my wife Nancy. She had been home that year with a new baby while I was on the road. We flew commercial to the Virgin Islands. The Secretary came in a few days later on an Air Force jet. In St. Croix, the Secretary spoke at a convention of the National Association of State Departments of Agriculture. The Park Service gave us a tour of reefs on a Park Service boat from the Buck Island Reef National Monument. From St. Croix we flew to Freeport, where the Secretary gave a speech before the Peanut Manufacturers and Nut Salters Association convention.

Albuquerque

While on one of the trips to Albuquerque, New Mexico, in 1972, we were waiting for a large function at the Albuquerque Convention Center where the Secretary was to be the speaker that evening. We had a block of rooms at the Downtowner Hotel in Albuquerque. Secretary and Mrs. Butz were in one room; Don Brock, the secretary's personal aide, Jack Neese, the bodyguard from the USDA Office of the Inspector General, and I were in other rooms.

Earlier in the day I had called my friend Forrest Putman, the FBI assistant special agent in charge in Albuquerque at the time. I had told him that I wanted to get some Indian jewelry for my wife Nancy while I was in New Mexico, and we had little time. He volunteered that some of his agents worked on the Indian reservations where such jewelry originated, and they kept an assortment of items for sale to visitors at the FBI office. He said he would send an agent over later.

We were in our individual rooms when an FBI agent knocked on the door of what he thought was my room but was instead that of Secretary Butz and Mrs. Butz. When the Secretary opened the door, the agent flipped his FBI credentials and said, "FBI, I've got the jewelry." He then walked past the Secretary and dumped the contents of a Seagram's liquor cloth bag full of turquoise jewelry onto Butz's bed. Secretary Butz did not know what to think, only that he was probably being framed. Word quickly came to me of the mix-up. Don Brock and I went to Butz's hotel room to recover the situation. Don and I purchased several items. Secretary Butz, who died in 2008 at age 96, often joked about the FBI being jewel thieves.

After the 1972 Presidential Campaign was over, I spent six months in the General Counsel's office at USDA before leaving and starting my own law practice.

My 34-Year Love Affair with the Army

I graduated from Latta High School, a rural country school near Ada, Oklahoma, in 1954. I started college that fall, but the military draft was still on. Several of my classmates joined the Navy or went into some other military service immediately out of high school.

When Congress enacted the Reserve Forces Act of

1957, my cousin, Theron Simpson, and I joined the 986th Field Artillery Battalion, an Army Reserve artillery unit located in a storefront on Main Street in Ada, Oklahoma. The new law required six months of active duty plus an obligation of six years in the Army Reserve.

Theron and I reported to Fort Chaffee, Arkansas, for basic training. Two others from Ada, Jerry Serber, and Gene Thomas, joined us. At Fort Chaffee, our company commander was Captain Richard H. Thompson. Captain Thompson had walked into Germany in World War II as a sergeant in an infantry division and stayed in the Army after receiving a commission. I would cross paths with him 30 years later. Captain Thompson and the cadre had us running up and down hills at Fort Chaffee growling like tigers. We were called "Thompson's Tigers." I recall the ten-mile marches with bags of flour being tossed along the route by a low flying aircraft to simulate real bombs.

After basic training, we all went to Fort Sill, Oklahoma, for Artillery Survey and Advanced Artillery Survey schools, now obsolete programs replaced by satellites and GPS. Later, I would attend one summer camp with the 986th back at Fort Sill before I moved to Norman, Oklahoma, in the fall of 1958 to return to the University of Oklahoma. I had previously completed one semester there in 1954.

I joined the Oklahoma City Police Department (OCPD) and transferred my reserve affiliation to the Military Police (MP) Company of the 95th Infantry Division. The 95th was a large Army Reserve unit headquartered in Oklahoma City. This unit conducted its annual summer camps at Fort Chaffee, Arkansas. We police officers in this MP unit taught most of the classes and were given great leeway. Often, when working the 3PM to 11PM police shift, we could just go by on drill nights and sign in for the attendance credit.

By 1961, I had moved up to the rank of sergeant. That same year, I obtained a college degree in math and physics at Central State College, now the University of Central Oklahoma (UCO). My company commander, Captain John R. Robertson, told me that he had a second lieutenant slot that he wanted to put me in for. I received a direct commission in August 1961 as a second lieutenant in the Military Police Corps, U.S. Army Reserve.

In the same month I became an MP officer, I started at the Oklahoma City University Law School at night and was also recruited by the FBI. The FBI was hiring science majors with law enforcement experience at the time. My appointment with the FBI in January 1962 was conditioned on transfer to the Standby Reserve. I was promoted to both first lieutenant and to captain in the Standby Reserve while an FBI agent. I had read the fine print on how to stay active and was able to get my fifty retirement points a year, mostly through extension courses. As an enlisted man I had completed the Special Investigations Course from the Military Police School. While in the FBI, I simultaneously completed the Military Police Career Course by correspondence and the Industrial College of the Armed Forces Course while an FBI Agent. I also completed a law degree by attending four different law schools.

When I left the FBI in October of 1969, I went from a GS-12 FBI Agent to a GS-15 in another agency in one day. I wanted to get back into a troop unit. The Vietnam War was on and most of the Reserve's units were heavily staffed with folks trying to stay out of Vietnam limiting vacancies. I first applied to the 10th Military Law Center, a unit I would later command. I was rejected because at that point I was a very senior captain and would soon be promoted to major with more limitations on vacancies. I tried to get other paid drill slots in the D.C. area without success. At that time, I was the executive assistant to the administrator of the Farmers Home Administration, the banking agency in the U.S. Department of Agriculture. One day I was complaining to Jack Sprague, who was an assistant administrator. Jack had been a World War II veteran and was then retired from the Army Reserve. He had served in a reserve unit called the 352nd Civil Affairs unit. I told him about my difficulty in finding a billet in a reserve unit. He looked at his watch and asked, "How much time have you got?" I said, "All you need."

We went out the front door of the South Agriculture Building and caught a cab over to the office of the National Rural Electric Cooperative Association, headed by Robert Partridge. The organization had strong ties to USDA. Partridge happened to be an Army Reserve brigadier general and the commander of the 352nd Civil Affairs Command. This Command had subordinate units that included the 300th Civil Affairs Group and the 354th Civil Affairs Brigade. That afternoon I was in a paid drill slot in the Legal Section of the 300th Civil Affairs Group at Riverdale, Maryland.

I transferred from the Military Police Branch to the Judge Advocate General's Corps (JAG) branch, as I now had a law degree and was a member of the Bar. My enlisted men at the 300th read like "Who's Who" of the Washington federal government legal establishment. They were all lawyers. I had Specialist Six Charlie Curtis as my chief legal clerk. He was the chief counsel for the House Interstate and Foreign Commerce Committee and later Secretary of Energy. I had Private First-Class Richard (Dick) Janis, a Harvard lawyer, who would later become Bert Lance's lawyer in that scandal in the Carter Administration and Hakim's lawyer in the Iran-Contra matter in the Reagan Administration. Specialist 3 Hugh Yarrington was the general counsel to the Bureau of National Affairs. I had assistant U.S. attorneys and SEC officials as well as Congressional aides and associates in large law firms. One, Specialist 3 Mark Wolf, would later be the Chief Federal Judge in Boston.

My enlisted men were bored to tears doing menial tasks at the Reserves center. They became haircut and discipline problems. To cover myself, I wanted to get them out of the reserve center. The active-duty Army JAGs hated to do legal assistance. I met with the staff judge advocate for the Military District of Washington and convinced him to let us staff his active Army legal assistance offices with my Army Reserve lawyers on weekends. I put them in suits and ties and let them do legal work. They loved every minute of it. I remember PFC Dick Janis coming up to my office at Fort Myer to ask, "What's a BG?" He was doing a will for a brigadier general who had no idea that a private first class was his lawyer. When the commander of that unit, Colonel Einar Windingland, retired, the only significant thing they could put in the brochure of his accomplishments during his tenure was Major George's legal assistance project at Fort McNair, Fort Myer, and Walter Reed.

The civil affairs units were military government units patterned after the occupation forces in Germany and Japan after World War II. After Vietnam, the Reserves were getting involved in what was called "mutual support" with active military units in the 1970s. As a result, the eight officers in the unit that were not overweight, me being one of them, were shipped down to Fort Bragg for various military exercises. I eventually parlayed that into a transfer to the 354th Civil Affairs Brigade, which was the next higher unit and was promoted to lieutenant colonel.

I moved up from there to be the staff judge advocate for the 352nd Civil Affairs Command and was promoted to full colonel. We conducted our summer camps at Camp A.P. Hill and Camp Pickett in Virginia, Indiantown Gap Military Reservation in Pennsylvania, and other boring spots. One year, due to budget cuts that eliminated travel, I took my legal section to the District of Columbia Corporation counsel's office, where we served our two weeks of active duty as D.C. government lawyers.

General Robert Partridge retired as commander of the 352nd Civil Affairs Command and was replaced by Brigadier General Wayne Jackson. By coincidence, Wayne was an ex-Tulsa, Oklahoma, police officer. He was also the chief probation officer of the U. S Courts. I, on the other hand, was a former Oklahoma City police officer. Wherever Wayne went afterwards, he took me along like his American Express Card. When he was transferred to command the 97th Army Reserve Command at Fort Meade, Maryland, for his second star, I went along as his staff judge advocate. The Judge Advocate General of the Army assigns JAG officers, and they had someone else they wanted assigned there. General Jackson told them, "If you don't pick Colonel George, I won't fill the slot." We had 14,000 reservists scattered from Maine to Florida and more aircraft than most airlines. We had special forces units, hospital units, aviation units, supply units, all of which generated a fair number of legal problems.

Lieutenant Colonel Bert Smith, my Deputy, had been a Vietnam War helicopter pilot and knew the Army much better than I. We made an effective team. I handled politics, and he handled most of the law stuff. We had three-year tenures in some of the troop-unit assignments.

I ended up in the office of the Judge Advocate General at the Pentagon. My title there was chief of litigation "IMA," which meant individual military assignment. This is a designation for reserve officers who are backsups for their active-duty counterpart and who would be their replacement if needed. While in this assignment, I also served on the active Army full colonel promotion boards for one year.

In 1989, I was attending the Association of U.S. Army Convention in Washington, D.C., which I attended annually to pick up a retirement point. I noticed the chart on the wall was a picture of the Secretary of the Army along with pictures of all the "warlords," the four-star generals. One of them happened to be my company commander from Fort Chaffee, Arkansas, in 1957. He was now Commander of the Army Materiel Command (AMC). Anything that the Army built or bought, General Richard H. Thompson oversaw it. He then had a $33 billion budget.

The only person I knew at the AMC at that time was the staff judge advocate, Colonel James McCune. The Army materiel command was often referred to as a million civilians. The command had a GS-18 general counsel. I copied pages from my book from Fort Chaffee, Arkansas, in 1957, with Captain Thompson and his staff, along with me and one hundred other privates, and sent a copy to Colonel McCune with a note, "Jim, is this the same guy?" About three days later, I received a call from the colonel. He was excited. He reported that he had taken my material to the general's office, and the general wanted me to come over for lunch at the AMC Headquarters in Alexandria, Virginia. What I did not know at the time was that the colonel had never met the four-star general. Four-stars talk to three-stars who talk to two-stars, and he was a mere colonel. So, from that point on he was riding on my coattails.

I went over to the AMC building in Alexandria, where McCune and I had a great lunch with General Thompson. I told them that the main thing that I remembered about Fort Chaffee, Arkansas, in 1957 was that he had us running up and down hills growling like tigers. He called us all "Thompson's Tigers." With that, the old general beamed and began telling stories about how all the people in his 40 years in the military who worked for him were "Thompson's Tigers." They had "Thompson's Tigers" t-shirts and so forth.

After that meeting, General Thomason and his wife Pat often invited my wife Nancy and me to his quarters at Fort McNair for various parties and for 4th of July celebrations. We could see the fireworks at the Washington Monument from his backyard at Fort McNair. When I put my late wife Nancy's ashes in Arlington National Cemetery, he and Pat were there. He told me he was on a military sales mission in Iran at the time the American Embassy was taken over. The Iranian military smuggled him out of the country on a British passport. A three-star general at the time, he would have been quite a catch for the militants who took over the US embassy.

On various occasions in the 1980s, I would be called to active duty for different projects or to sit on boards. While out of a paid drill assignment in a unit for a brief time, I needed to get my two weeks active duty over with. I called my new best friend, Colonel Jim McCune, at AMC, who now knew the four-star general because of Colonel George. I asked him to set me up in his office, as I needed to get my two-week obligation out of the way. He said, "No problem. We will set you up in the general's office." The next call I received was from Major General Hugh Overholt, the Army Judge Advocate General (TJAG). A four-star general had requested an Army Reserve JAG officer by name from the Reserve Component Personnel Center. The two-star generals get a bit insecure when four-star generals request their JAG officers by name from the control group. He wanted to know what the [expletive deleted] I was pulling. I told him, "Gee, boss, I'm just trying to get my two weeks out of the way."

While I was on active duty at the materiel command, they had completed a big investigation of gratuities for defense contractors, which they wanted to resolve. Contractors ran ammunition plants and so forth. When the active-duty military guys would come to the remote plants, the contractors might feed them lunch as a courtesy. Someone wanted to make a big stink that this was gratuities from the defense contractors. I pulled the reports together, did the briefings and buried it, which was just what they expected. Just because contractors might provide lunch to visiting military officers in out of the way remote locations does not make it a crime. I received an officer efficiency report (OER) from a four-star general that read, "Every day the Army doesn't make Colonel George a general the Army's a loser." That made me number two on about eight different reserve general officer slots.

Unfortunately, in the Reserves, one must get assigned to the position before the promotion. While I was backup on eight positions, no slot became vacant before mandatory removal finally took me out after 34 years. At this same time, my wife was going through breast cancer, and I was trying to do her lobbying job and my own legal and lobbying work too. It probably worked out for the best. For my last two years, I was the commander of the 10th Military Law Center, the unit that I had tried to get into in 1969 but was rejected.

I am a graduate of the U.S. Army War College, and among other awards I received the Legion of Merit, one of the highest ones without being shot at.

Staff Judge Advocate Colonel Charlie Murray, the military equivalent to a general counsel for the Rapid Deployment Joint Task Force (RDJTF), now Central Command, would ask me to fill in for him when his trips to the middle east conflicted with military exercises in the U.S. I would receive orders to go to MacDill Air Force Base, Florida, or Fort Bragg, North Carolina, to be the legal advisor to the RDJTF commander, Lieutenant General Robert Kingston and his deputy, General Carl Stiner, and to fill in for Colonel Murray. This was heady stuff for a street lawyer in D.C. Few reserve officers have those opportunities. As with doctors, active and reserve JAG officers are interchangeable.

While I was SJA for the 97th Army Reserve Command at Fort Meade, the 10th Military Law Center was one of our subordinate units. It had become a bit of a haven for slackers compared to our other ARCOM units. We had thousands of reservists in our Special Forces, hospital, supply, aviation, and other units gainfully employed with the Army Reserve, but these guys and gals at the 10th MLC, instead of training in their specialties—such as courts martial, international law, administrative law, and the like—were doing legal assistance and going home at noon. General Jackson, my ARCOM Commander, told me to get that unit gainfully employed or he would use the money for his rapid deployment units. This was just what I wanted to hear.

I recruited Colonel John Early MacDonald, a JAG officer from the Virginia Army National Guard. John was an Armor Branch officer early on in his career and wore combat boots with buckles. He wanted the job, and I wanted him to have the job. He wreaked havoc, cleaned out all the dead wood and got the unit turned around. About two weeks into his tenure, I received a long letter on State Department stationery from one of the detachment commanders, a close friend, and then the chief consular officer at the State Department. He was complaining about Colonel McDonald. It confirmed that McDonald was doing just what I wanted him to do.

By coincidence, John was also the Vice President and claims counsel for Lawyers Title Insurance Corporation in Richmond, Virginia. I ended up as a lawyer for Lawyers Title and made significant money for myself and my law firm representing them for various cases. I tended to resolve many matters and questions for my law firm, thanks to my numerous JAG contacts. I had fifty representatives from nearly every agency in D.C. working for me one weekend per month—the Department of Justice, the U.S. Army Corps of Engineers, Resolution

Trust Corporation, the Federal Communications Commission, the State Department, et al.

Practicing Law

In 1973, after the excitement of working in the 1972 presidential campaign, I was bored with working in the USDA General Counsel's Office. I was able to get my job abolished, receive 13 weeks of severance pay, drew out my federal retirement that had accrued from the FBI and USDA, and started law practice in Washington D.C. as a sole practitioner. I shared offices with other individual lawyers early on.

I had assumed, having spent a year in an airplane with the Secretary of Agriculture, that agribusiness clients would be seeking me to represent them. Unfortunately, that did not happen for a couple of years. Fortunately, though, I was staffing the Army legal assistance offices on weekends at Fort McNair, Fort Myers, and Walter Reed Hospital with my Army Reserve lawyers. As a result, I enjoyed all manner of referrals for general practice cases: personal injury cases, real estate settlements, divorce cases, bankruptcy cases and the like. It was the "ash and trash" of law practice, not always that glamorous, but it paid. Starting fresh, I still never made less than I had made with the government. Eventually the good cases came with Pizza Hut, Wendy's, and Frito Lay, et al. I kept my hand in general practice as I enjoyed both helping people and the variety. For a while, after she completed law school, my wife Nancy and I practiced together.

Miles and Stockbridge, a large Baltimore law firm approached me to open a Washington office for them, and Nancy went out on her own. I took the Washington office from one attorney (me) to eleven attorneys. The law firm had expanded quickly, and shortly after opening a D.C. office, the firm opened offices in Fairfax, Virginia, and Rockville, Maryland. My overhead, across the street from the White House, was much higher. We were often living off the same clients. I was always under the gun from the home office. I assembled a team of great lawyers, including Greg Luce, who went to head the healthcare law section for Skadden Arps, Nina Novak, John Rainbolt, Richard Vernon, James H. Davidson, and Timothy Battle, to name a few. I even had as a new associate Kathy Courtney, who went on to be the Governor of New York (as Kathy Hochul).

Each firm handles partner compensation differently. At Miles, the partner compensation was based upon personal billings and re-set every other year. Roughly, if one billed $400K annually, the compensation was $200K. If one billed $400K and brought in another $400K in work for others, as I did, the compensation was still only $200K, and we were stuck with that number for two years. Eventually the rapid expansion caught up with the firm and Richard Vernon and I particularly got shafted. We coasted for the next two years and moved to other firms. Rich went to Lerch, Early, and I took my clients to the D.C. office of Gage & Tucker, a large Kansas City firm, which with a merger became Lathrop & Gage. My first month I billed $38,000. I was lucky to have a great client base. If one gets the work, there are plenty of smart people to help do it. I surrounded myself with those. There were great attorneys with the Lathrop & Gage firm, and I stayed there until moving to Santa Fe in 2001.

One of my first cases when I "hung out a shingle" and started law practice in Washington, D.C. in 1973 was the case of Lieutenant John Glover. A former FBI Agent friend, Tom Sullivan, referred the case to me. Tom was the legislative assistant for Congressman Sam Steiger of Arizona.

Glover was a native of Ash Fork, Arizona. He had attended the New Mexico Military Institute in Roswell. He was attending the Infantry Officer Basic School at Fort Benning, Georgia, as the Vietnam War was beginning to wind down. He was accused of cheating on a physical fitness test merely because his score card from the test was lost. He was summarily dismissed from active duty. He was the only son of Robert Glover, a Civil Engineer in Ash Fork, Arizona. The two of them came to Washington to meet with me.

After doing a considerable amount of investigation that I would never have undertaken had I had something better to do, I determined that the Army was trying to cut back at that point and preferred to weed out officers who were not West Point graduates as the Vietnam War was winding down. We non-West Point officers refer to this phenomenon as the West Point Protective Association in action. In any event, the Army was looking for anything they might use to get rid of officers. Glover was already Airborne Qualified. He had gone to Airborne School while at New Mexico Military Institute. He had no problem with physical fitness. He could probably do pushups with only one arm. Additionally, I determined that, legally, because of his prior service with ROTC, several administrative remedies had been denied him.

I took the case before the Army Board for Correction of Military Records at the Pentagon and obtained a reversal. He was reinstated to active duty with all his back pay restored. John went on to finish a career in the military. He at one point worked for one of my former neighbors, Major General John Stanford, then the commander of the Military Traffic Management Command in Oakland, California. Glover later earned a PhD and worked as a historian for the Department of Army at Hurlburt Field in Florida. His expertise included documenting the Afghan and Iraq Wars.

Cat Custody

Early in my law practice I represented a Congressional staffer's wife who was involved in a contentious divorce with her Congressional staffer husband. They ran up over $6,000 on each side, a lot of money then, fighting over custody of two cats. We eventually reached a property settlement agreement in which we arranged joint custody of the cats, and they agreed to split the veterinary bills.

Walter Wadewitz

Walter R. (Wally) Wadewitz was referred to me by Walter Miller, a stockbroker friend. Both Wally and his wife were survivors of the Bataan Death March. He was an Army officer, and she was an Army nurse. Initially, they just wanted to get Wally admitted to a good Veterans Administration hospital in another part of the country, preferably in Arizona. Both later died in the 1990s.

As I got into the facts with them, I learned Wally had

been diagnosed with throat cancer at the Walter Reed Army Medical Center. This was back when they did not really know what they were dealing with. The doctors decided to bus him over to the Bethesda Naval Hospital to give him some of the "healing ray" from radiation treatment. They wiped out the cancer, but he eventually became a quadriplegic as a result.

My wife Nancy had experienced a minor stroke at one point and had been examined by Dr. Juan James, a neurologist in Alexandria, Virginia. I sent Wally's file over to Dr. James and asked if he would review it. After a review, he opined that Wally's treatment with radiation had really done severe damage.

James Otway was a lawyer working for me at the time. We filed a Federal Tort Claim Act (FTCA) case against the government. In FTCA cases, one must make an administrative claim first before filing a lawsuit. In Wally's case, the six-month statutory period for response from the government passed, which is typical, so we filed suit in the U.S. District Court in Maryland. The information we obtained indicated that Wally had received over 6,000 rads on his spinal column while treating throat cancer. Most medical experts at the time considered 5,000 rads to be negligence. They had the Navy equivalent of a private first class making the calculations. Anything that could have been done wrong was done wrong. For example, they placed a lead shield between the radiation beams to his throat and his spinal column. Their own portal films showed the edge of the spinal column, the most sensitive part of the spine, was sticking out beyond the width of the metal block.

Radiation goes out like a flashlight beam, smaller at the start and larger at the end. We also determined that they had not gapped the fields. As a result, he was getting a double dose of radiation in those fields where the radiation beams overlapped.

The government filed a motion to dismiss, and the federal judge granted it. We filed a motion for reconsideration, and we rolled Wally and his wheelchair into the courtroom. To our surprise, the judge reinstated the case after seeing Wally. There were many problems on our side of the case. The judge just gave us a chance to settle the case. There was the two-year statute of limitations on the federal tort claims issue, as this begins to run from the point when he knew or should have known what caused his injury, and we were arguably past that. I brought in friends Dick Janis and Henry Schulke, both of whom had just left the Justice Department and had gone into private practice on their own. With their help, we settled the case for $1 million dollars. Had we not been past the statute of limitations problem, the settlement would have been several times higher than that.

In federal tort claims cases, attorney fees are limited to 25 % of the settlement, so Janis and Schulke got $125K, and I got $125K. Wally got the rest. Until he and his wife came to my office, they had no idea they had a potential claim. They just wanted me to get Wally into a better Veterans Administration Hospital in some other part of the country.

Paul Zukowski

Paul was referred to me by a friend and his brother, Dick Zukowski, who was the vice-president of the American Indian National Bank. Paul Zukowski at one time had been the world's champion roller skater. He had teamed up with an individual named Dwight Dunton. Part of their deal was that Dunton would fund the costs of building a roller-skating rink near Andrews Air Force Base, and Zukowski would get it up and running. Once Dunton had skimmed enough out of the business to get back his original investment, he would give Zukowski title to one half of the land and buildings, worth several hundred thousand dollars. Once that threshold was reached, Dunton refused to add Zukowski's name to the title.

We went to trial in the U.S. District Court of the Eastern District of Virginia before District Court Judge John A. MacKenzie. He was a federal judge from Norfolk, Virginia, and was sent to Alexandria for this trial. Judge MacKenzie wrote a nine-page opinion finding in our favor. He started off with, "Mr. Zukowski and Mr. Dunton had numerous business deals over the years, during which each defrauded the other. It is these claims and counterclaims that now burden this court." Then he went on for nine pages about what rotten no-good jerks they both were, but that Dunton was a little worse than our guy. As a result, Zukowski was awarded half interest in the land and buildings.

During the trial, the managers of the skating rink, fortunately for us, had kept careful records to cover their butts. Mr. Dunton would come by and pick up a bag of cash consisting of the receipts for the week, and for example, it might be $6,000. When Dunton deposited the money in the bank, he might deposit only $3,000. Dunton subsequently went to federal prison for income tax evasion.

Shortly after the trial, we learned that Zukowski and Dunton had gotten together to make a deal to cut us out of the attorney fees. Jim Otway and I served Notice of Attorney Liens on everyone that we could find connected to the matter. Virginia has a strong Attorney's Lien Statute, and this put them on notice of our claim. It squelched their secret deal. Then we sued Zukowski to collect the attorney fees of some $90,000.

I was swamped with other matters at the time. My wife Nancy, who had just gotten her law degree, prepared for the hearing. I moved her special admission to handle this case because she was not a member of the Virginia Bar. In those days, there were few women in the courtroom. The podium was taller than she was at 5'2", and the other two lawyers were each tall. The Judge kept calling the lawyers up to the bench. Nancy was so short that she could not see over the podium, so she would get up behind the bench with the federal judge each time, which was unprecedented. All during the trial the Judge kept referring to her as "little lady." I was amused, despite what now may be considered a sexist form of address. And I was proud that she won. The court awarded the judgment in full for our attorney fees, and we promptly filed the judgment in every place that Zukowski had real estate of record. We eventually got paid in full.

Boren House

I met my late wife, Nancy Lou Whorton, in 1963. She was a college student at East Central State College in Ada, Oklahoma. Her roommate was Molly Shi, whom I had known all her life. Molly had arranged a blind date for us. Molly would later go on to marry David Boren, who at that time was the Governor of Oklahoma. When he was elected to the United States Senate, they came to Washington. At that time, my wife had a real estate license. She found them a new townhouse across Shirley Highway from the Army Navy Country Club.

David had been through a divorce and was written up as the poorest of the one hundred Senators. Nancy waived her real estate commission, and I was to handle the real estate settlement. I took the then Senator-elect to see Marty Schneider, who owned Northern Virginia Savings & Loan. He was a friend of Deke Deloach, a benefactor of mine from FBI days, and a long-time contact in the FBI. I introduced the governor to Marty as the new Senator from Oklahoma. I told him the Senator needed a home loan for a certain amount. Marty, who owned the S&L, did not have to worry about a loan committee. He promptly said, "No problem, Senator, here is the deal." He never considered any financials. There really were not any. There was no delay and no forms to cope with.

When it came time for the real estate settlement, I began totaling the numbers and found that I was about $2,000 short on necessary closing costs. The client really does not know what happened after that, but I knew how to make things work. I called my friends Joe Hillings with Fluor Corporation and Dick Sewell with Florida Power & Light. We put together an Energy Breakfast at the University Club. We figured we could pass the "straight face test" with that one since he was on the Energy Committee of the Southern Governors Conference and still a governor. We charged the lobbyist attendees $100 each. I had the Senator-elect speak at breakfast, and we gave the attendees the opportunity to meet him. I walked away with $2,600 after Dick Sewell picked up the tab for breakfast. I now had ample money to close the real estate transaction.

When David left the Senate to go back to be president of the University of Oklahoma, he gave me a Power of Attorney. I sold the house and sent him the money. Over the years we had refinanced it several times for tuition money for his children by a previous marriage. It sold for a a huge gain.

Daniella Laufer

My friend Stanley McKiernan, a Nixon Family lawyer in Los Angeles, periodically referred to me unique cases. One involved a metal spice box full of charred $100 bills, which I took over to the Treasury Department. The technicians pieced together the charred remains, and I was handed a check for $75,000. The client had a story about how this came out of a hotel fire in Korea. I did not want to ask more.

For several months, Stanley had urged me to take a case involving the sister of one of his clients, Mrs. Daniella Laufer. Her ex-husband was an international wheeler-dealer and a resident of Hungary. He claimed to be a survivor of Auschwitz. She worked for SAKs or Nieman Marcus, in Tyson's Corner, in northern Virginia. They had been married and divorced each other twice, over a prolonged period.

In her last divorce, Mrs. Laufer had obtained an order for alimony in the District of Columbia. The arrears had already been reduced to a judgment, and Mr. Laufer was over $100,000 behind. My mission was to collect the alimony judgment from a guy living in Hungary. I saw this as a loser from the start. Only after McKiernan kept urging me to take the case did I do so. I finally told him I would take it on a 50% contingency, but never expected to see a dime.

At one point Mr. Laufer had been a real estate developer building houses in the District of Columbia and had taken back promissory notes when he sold the properties to residents. He had put together a deal for a resort in Ocho Rios, Jamaica, from which he allegedly made a lot of money. He had taken up with a girlfriend who had been the administrative assistant of Senator Mike Gravel of Alaska. She was now living with Laufer in Hungary.

I received a tip that the girlfriend was visiting her daughter in Washington. I promptly served a notice to take her deposition. She refused to show up for the deposition. I went into D.C. Superior Court with a motion to compel before Superior Court Judge Colleen Kollar-Kotelly, a no-nonsense Judge. (She later became a federal judge.) To my pleasant surprise, the judge entered the alimony judgment against the girlfriend for her refusal to submit to discovery. Suddenly, I had a judgment against someone who owned a house in the District of Columbia. The house was occupied by a German television executive who was paying her $2,500 a month rent.

I promptly served a Writ of Attachment on the television executive, so he now had to make his rent payments to me. I now had money to fund the lawsuit. I happened to be at a party in D.C. one evening and ran into a friend, Mark Bloom. I asked Mark if he was the same Mark Bloom that had bought property from Mr. Laufer. I had seen that name in some of the documents I had obtained. Mark, who was an assistant to Secretary of the Treasury, Charlie Walker, lit into a diatribe about what a rotten, ugly, no-goodnik Mr. Laufer was. He claimed he had just gotten a notice from the bank directing him to start paying his mortgage payments directly to Mr. Laufer instead of to the bank. I promptly served a Writ of Attachment on Mark, requiring him to send the mortgage payments to me. I later determined that a bunch of money from the Ocho Rios deal had been received, whereby Laufer could pay off his loan with the bank and retrieve his promissory notes that he had placed as collateral.

My client ran into Laufer's lawyer, who apologized to her and explained that substantial money from the Ocho Rios real estate development that Laufer built had passed through the lawyer's trust account and had been sent to Mr. Laufer in Hungary. I promptly subpoenaed the lawyer to take his deposition. He refused, claiming attorney-client privilege. At least I was getting two or three thousand dollars a month from the German TV executive along with Mark's mortgage payments that he had been sending to Laufer. I really did not think Mr. Laufer would show from Hungary for a status hearing. To my surprise, when my client and I arrived at the D.C. Superior Courthouse, he was there representing himself as his own lawyer. The hearing went on for several days during which the judge might hold a one- or two-hour session and then recess to handle other cases.

Laufer tried to call his prior lawyer as a witness. I explained to the judge that I had tried to depose this fellow, and he had refused, claiming attorney-client privilege. The judge recessed the hearing and told Laufer's lawyer to go outside and talk to me. I then learned that Mr. Laufer had the promissory notes now in his possession. I asked the judge to direct Laufer to bring the notes to court the following day, which he did. My client was quite a problem, but he had married her twice. She would jerk my arm and contradict me at times when I was trying to speak to the court. At the end of the second day session, the judge asked, "What am I supposed to do with these promissory notes?" I told him to give them to the Clerk of Court. He and his courtroom clerk huddled, and they eventually turned the notes over to the official court clerk for safekeeping.

The next day, our third day of hearing, it so happened that there had been a huge water break in downtown D.C. I could not get to my office, because the streets were all flooded in that vicinity. My wife was recovering from breast cancer, so I could not use her as a process server to serve a Writ of Attachment to seize the promissory notes. My friend Paul Lamberth, whom I often used, was out of pocket. However, when I walked in the D.C. Superior Courthouse on Fifth Street that morning I ran into an old friend, Raymond Jacobsen. Ray was a brigadier general in the Army Reserve. He was also known as a "Fifth Street lawyer," as lawyers are known to hang around the courthouse to handle public defender cases as needed. I said, "Come on, Ray, you're gonna be a process server." We went up to the clerk's office and asked the clerk to come out to the counter. I had Ray serve him with a Writ of Attachment, attaching the promissory notes that the clerk was holding. It is probably one of the few times that a Writ of Attachment has been served on a clerk of court.

The next day of the hearing, the Judge told Mr. Laufer that his hands were tied, that Mr. George had attached Laufer's promissory notes held by the clerk. We ended the hearing. I was getting the girlfriend's mortgage payments from the German television executive tenant of her townhouse and getting Mark Bloom's mortgage payments to one the several promissory notes the clerk was now holding. I now had complete control of the situation. Mr. Laufer promptly paid the back-alimony judgment. I got paid $50,000 for an impossible case that I had no chance of winning.

Grass Roots Constitutional Law

The closest thing to a constitutional law case I would have involved representation of the want ad newspaper, Thrifty Nickel. The company came to me to represent them in a case in the city of Falls Church, VA. The city was after them over several thousand dollars of back taxes. If it were an advertising circular it was taxable but if it was a newspaper, it would be taxation of speech and thus prohibited. I went to trial in the municipal court in Falls Church trying to prove it was a newspaper. I kept introducing copies and pointing out civic announcements, etc. The municipal judge sat on a decision for over six months before ruling against us. I then took the case to the next level in the Circuit Court in Arlington. After another lengthy trial, and introducing numerous copies of our publication, which became a big stack of paper on the Judges' bench, both sides rested. The judge turned to his courtroom clerk and asked, "What am I supposed to do with all these newspapers?"

FBI Agents Association

The FBI Agents Association is the organization of current FBI agents (FBIAA). While not a union, the organization is interested in anything that impacts FBI agents' jobs, salaries, and benefits.

Ed Bethune, a former Congressman from Arkansas, a former FBI agent. and a longtime friend, was their lobbyist and lawyer in Washington. One day Ed called to tell me that he wanted to sail his sailboat around the world. He told me that he had this little client, the FBIAA. He indicated that there was not much going on but wanted me to cover for him while he was away. I assured him that I would be happy to do so. Subsequently, Larry Langberg, the president and Susan Lloyd, the secretary of the association, came to Washington to meet with me to talk about their issues.

At that time, the association was supporting legislation to do away with the mandatory age 55 retirement for FBI agents, and to obtain premium pay in the larger high-cost cities. For example, an FBI agent in Liberal, Kansas, as a GS-13, was affluent while the same agent in Los Angeles may be near poverty because of the excessive cost of living. The mandatory retirement mandate was wiping out the institutional memory in many offices by losing the most experienced agents.

I had several meetings on Capitol Hill with key representatives and staff. Ed Bethune had not been gone more than a couple of weeks when everything came together. I was able to get their legislation through Congress to address these interests. The association was quite happy with this result. They even gave me a bonus of $3,000, even though I had been paid an hourly rate for a few weeks. An unintended consequence of this was that it reportedly shut down new agents' classes for about three years.

Lawyers Title Insurance Corporation

Lawyers Title Insurance Corporation (LTIC) insures titles to real estate. I picked up this client after recruiting the Vice President and claims counsel, John McDonald, to head the 10th Military Law Center. This was one of the units in the 97th ARCOM where I was the staff judge advocate. We were both colonels in the Army's Judge Advocate General's Branch (JAG) at the time. This was a unit that I later commanded adjacent to Andrews Air Force Base. John was in the Virginia Army National Guard, and we needed someone from the outside to shake up this unit.

My law firm and I subsequently represented LTIC on several projects involving expensive screw-ups. We had one in Padre Island, Texas, where Lawyers Title had insured the title for a new luxury resort. With the foreclosures in the 1970s, an additional title search was conducted which revealed that the original title company who handled the first real estate settlement and title search had missed a spoilage easement held by the U.S. Army Corps of Engineers. Spoilage is what they dredge up to clear ship channels. It is the smelly mud, muck, clam shells, beer cans, and the like. You can imagine this yuck being rained down upon those new 580SL Mercedes with the tops down at the resort covered by the easement. So, it was a big, costly screw up.

One of my Army JAG officers was Lieutenant Colonel (LTC) Frank Carr, the chief of litigation for the U.S. Army Corps of Engineers. He coached me on how to fix this title problem and gave me an entrée and an approach. We then obtained other land that the Corps of Engineers could use for spoilage and traded it to them, solving a major title problem. Millions of dollars were saved, and because of my Army connections, I am only one of a tiny few who could have resolved it.

Another case involved the purchase by Lawyers Title Insurance Company of a title company in Las Vegas, Nevada. They bought themselves into a major problem. We learned that there was potential mortgage fraud in many of the loans that had been closed by this local title company. Lawyers Title got sued by the government under the False Claims Act for $100 million. I worked on this matter for a couple of years. We had lawyers involved in the litigation in Las Vegas while I was trying to resolve the case at the political level in Washington, D.C. My friend was the general counsel of Housing and Urban Development (HUD) at the time, Frank Keating. (Frank was not Keating of the Keating Five scandal in Arizona.) We both had been FBI agents, and he would later become Governor of Oklahoma.

Even though this was a HUD case, the Department of Justice (DOJ) was responsible for litigation or settling such cases. Frank did have authority to bring the DOJ lawyers over to HUD periodically. I would bring the lawyers in from Las Vegas, as we tried to resolve the claim. Eventually, we were able to settle the case for $9 million, a fraction of the original claim. I still thought that Lawyers Title was the victim and that they should not pay anything. I received a call shortly thereafter to meet my client, John McDonald. He had driven up from Richmond to have dinner with me in Alexandria, Virginia.

I was feeling bad about the settlement because I hated to see them give away all that money. What I did not understand at the time were the implications of this being a publicly held company. When they had a claim of $100 million, they had to disclose it to the shareholders, and it impacted the company stock price. They were looking at it from a completely different perspective. John proceeded to tell me what a wonderful job I had done in resolving that case. Even though I had been paid by the hour all along, he said, "Send me a bill for $75,000. If it is any more than that, I must get approval from higher up in the company." That is when I learned about value billing. He was a hero within the company, and he wanted to share with someone who made that happen.

A Unique Resolution

My friend Stanley McKiernan, a lawyer in Los Angeles, referred a matter to me which initially involved getting his client out of jail in Washington D.C. The client had been a professor with ties to Iran who taught at Belmont Abbey College in Charlotte, North Carolina. This was back when the Shah Mohammad Reza Pahlavi was in power. The professor was doing various investment deals in Iran with several high-powered investors with ties to his employer, Belmont Abbey College. These included prominent names like Luther Hodges, former North Carolina Governor and Secretary of Commerce. Later, when the Shah of Iran was deposed, the investors lost their money, and the professor left town in a hurry.

Several years later, the professor, then living in California, was with a group at the White House to present a gift to Vice President George Bush. When the White House security officials checked the National Crime Information Center database upon the group's entry, they found an old arrest warrant from Charlotte for fraud, and the professor was jailed. I was able to get him released from custody by posting bail and then grabbed my friend Dick Janis. We flew to Charlotte to meet with the prosecutor. Dick, a Harvard lawyer, had been a PFC in my legal section in a D.C. Army Reserve unit. He later was Bert Lance's lawyer in that scandal in the Carter Administration when Lance was head of the Office of Management and Budget, which was accused of corruption in 1977. He was later Albert Hakim's lawyer in the Iran-Contra matter in the Reagan Administration in 1987 involving arms sales to Iran and funding the Contras in Nicaragua. Dick did his former assistant-U.S.-attorney soft shoe, and I did my former FBI-agent soft shoe. We agreed to contribute $6,000 to Belmont Abbey College, and the prosecutor dropped the case.

Dr. Benjamin Franklin

In the 1970s, Benjamin Franklin was an Army doctor stationed at Walter Reed Army Hospital in Washington, D.C. He was a Black officer and had been living with a Black nurse for several months while assigned there. Upon receiving his orders transferring him to Fort Riley, Kansas, he came home to their apartment and said, "Baby, it's been swell." He then began carrying his clothes out of the apartment and putting them in the trunk of his car.

She was furious and proceeded to ram her car into his car, crushing his legs between the bumpers. He was in the Walter Reed Army Hospital for about six weeks as a patient while recovering from this injury. He finally limped out to Fort Riley for his new assignment. One of the first persons he met upon arrival was a U.S. Marshal who served him with legal papers for a suit to establish a common-law marriage in the District of Columbia, one of the few jurisdictions that still legally recognized common-law marriages. He requested that I represent him in court in this District of Columbia. We were eventually successful in prevailing on behalf of the doctor.

Football

In 1973, when I first began practicing law in Washington, D.C., I was contacted by an old friend who had been the commander of my Army Reserve unit in Oklahoma City, John R. Robertson, Jr. He was an oil and gas lawyer. He indicated that he planned to bring a client to Washington to bid on some federal oil and gas leases in Mississippi and Arkansas through the Bureau of Land Management (BLM). He wanted me to help, and I did not have much of a calendar to clear at that time. The client was a former jock with the University of Arkansas and was trying to get started in the oil business. The three of us spent three days shoulder to shoulder in a room in the Hilton Hotel in D.C., putting together bids.

These bids were mostly for drilling rights for oil and gas leases in national forests and public lands in the states of Mississippi and Arkansas. It was in the early days of computers. The client kept calling back to his home office to run the numbers we needed in assembling the bids. Once we finished the bids, my friend and the client went home. I took our bids to the BLM and submitted them. Fifteen years later, the client, Jerry Jones, bought the Dallas Cowboys football team. He was a nice guy then. That work, plus $100 dollars now, might get me a parking place at the AT&T Stadium where the Cowboys play.

American Indian National Bank

The American Indian National Bank (AINB) was set up in the early 1970s by General George Olmsted of Financial General. He thought the bank would be able to get deposits from Alaskan Indian claims money soon to be available at that time. He rammed it through the Comptroller Currency, which ruffled some feathers. It always received more than normal supervision as the regulators were skeptical of the institution. Once those Alaskan deposits did not come, Olmsted spun the bank off to the major Indian tribes.

AINB was located at 1701 Pennsylvania Avenue, NW in the same building as my law office. Bank officials asked me to come over and swear in the new board of directors since I was Notary. I had a tough time keeping a straight face as I read the lengthy oath of office to the assembled chiefs of the major Indian tribes, including Navaho, Sioux, Hopi, Cherokees, and the like. They stood there somberly with right hands raised. I was certainly out of place.

I parlayed that experience into doing collection cases and eventually ended up as the banks outside counsel. The small bank always had difficulty trying to serve nationwide in Indian country. It eventually merged with Metropolitan Bank, another small DC bank. I obtained the legal work for the merger for my Baltimore law firm and later moved my attorney checking and trust account deposits over to the new bank. One day my friend and favorite banker, Don Jacubec, initiated an urgent call telling me that the Metropolitan Bank was going under the following day, and I had better get my deposits out. I immediately did so. I did a fair amount of real estate settlements back then and often had several hundred thousand dollars in my attorney trust account from pending transactions. I would have been stuck personally with any losses of client's funds over the $100,000 FDIC guarantee. It is great to be lucky enough to have friends who look out for me.

No Good Deed Goes Unpunished: George F. Allen

This is about the first time I was naive enough to put my name on someone's estate papers. I do this about every 40 years.

I met George F. Allen, a staff director or administrative assistant for Florida Democratic Congressman Robert Sikes, when I handled a divorce for him from Shirley Lazonby in 1976. I was led to believe her to be his first wife. They had a young son, and Allen entered into a property settlement providing for a college education for this child. Shortly thereafter, George married Ellen, a young Congressional staff aide. George and Ellen then had one daughter, Mary Forest Allen. My wife and I saw them frequently over the next several years with dinners at their home or pursuant to real estate purchases and other legal issues. George then moved to the position of staff director of the House Armed Services Committee.

George called me one morning to inform me that he and Ellen were splitting. He was leaving on a Congressional trip out of the country with the Armed Services Committee members the next day. He wanted to make a new will. I explained that until he was divorced there was no way he could cut out Ellen, but he still insisted he wanted a new one. In obtaining the information, I asked whom he wanted as a personal representative. He could not think of anyone at the time and insisted that it be me. I told him that I did not usually do that sort of thing but agreed to do so under these urgent circumstances. I told him that as soon as he had his life straightened out, we should add another personal representative.

I printed off the will with the dispositions he desired and took a cab to his office at the House Armed Services Committee on Capitol Hill. We grabbed a couple of witnesses on his staff, he signed the will, and left for his trip the following day. I put the original in his file, and we each forgot about it.

George then went from being a Democratic staff director of the House Armed Services Committee to be a Republican Deputy Assistant Secretary of Defense for Congressional relations under the Reagan administration.

On a day I will never forget, in August 1988, I received a call at home at 7AM from Secretary of Defense Carlucci's office at the Pentagon. The caller informed me that George had died late the previous night on a C-5A flight to Europe. The caller wanted to know what I wanted to do with the body. I said, "What do you mean, do with the body?" The caller said that in every place in Allen's civilian records, he had indicated me as the person to contact in the case of emergency and that I was named as trustee for the young daughter on all his government paperwork. George was then in his late sixties. He had lied about his age to get into the Marine Corps in World War II at 15. After scurrying around that day, trying to get a handle on his affairs and making funeral arrangements, I discovered that he was living with one woman and was getting a hop on the U.S. Air Force flight to Europe to see another one. And I received a call from a third one indicating that she was supposed to drive him to Andrews Air Force Base for his flight, but George had told her that he was having a government driver take him.

I later learned that, on his flight to Europe that night, about an hour or so above the ocean, as they started to put the bunks down, Allen collapsed with a heart attack. The Air Force pilots landed this massive airplane in Gander, Newfoundland, where he was pronounced dead. Canadian law forbids removing the body from Canada under these circumstances, and this ordeal created a bit of an international incident. The pilots said, "Screw that," that he was a DoD official, and they took off with the body, bringing it back to Andrews Air Force Base. This was after waking folks for miles around by landing the huge plane.

As my day developed, I learned that what I had thought was wife number one was really wife number four. I went to his high-rise apartment building in Alexandria and told the manager that Mr. Allen had died the previous night, and I needed to gain access to his unit. The manager said, "Oh you are Peyton George. Here are the keys." My name was there just as with his government files. As it developed, he had five ex-wives and seven children who were scattered throughout the country. Most of the kids, ranging in age from 9 to 40, did not realize that they had siblings. George lived a very compartmentalized life. I found letters written to him from children to which he had never responded. One, whom he abandoned at birth, wrote, "Dear Dad, I am a tall girl. Is anyone in the family tall? Please write me." He saved letters but never responded. He would have a wife and child or two, then pack up, go to another location, and start all over again.

I arranged his funeral in Alexandria, Virginia. It was attended by most of his ex-wives, all his children, and twenty-seven members of Congress. Everybody loved George, especially the women. We gave him a proper send-off. Once I got into his financial affairs, I found that he had left all his government insurance and benefits to me as "Trustee for Mary Forest," nine years old at the time. But no trust agreement existed. There was little else, and the probate assets were under $40,000. As a result, the child from marriage number four, who was supposed to get a college education paid for, had an attorney but got little, and wife number five had an attorney. I was caught in the middle, and everyone was mad at me. I eventually let the minor children's mothers fight it out. We reached a court settlement on the disposition of the meager probate assets.

As an aside, after signing for the funeral, I discovered a limit on the percentage of probate assets that could be expended on funerals. I had some anxious moments as I had gone way over budget. I transferred the money I held as Trustee to Mary Forest to Ellen, the mother under the Uniform Gift to Minors Act. I got paid myself, but not much.

One of the items in George's estate was a new, but very dirty Toyota Cressida automobile. I took it to a detailing place to clean it inside and out, so that I could sell it. George was a very heavy smoker. When I came to retrieve it, one of the workers said that there was so much smoke residue and nicotine inside "that if that old boy ever ran out of cigarettes all he had to do was lick the glass."

Over the years, I tried to locate Mary Forrest, who was nine at the time of her father's death. In 2016, one of my letters paid off. I forwarded her a packet of personal items I had saved for years from his Pentagon office. She was in her thirties then and was grateful because she knew little about her father.

History Repeats Itself: Beverly Creighton Read

I realize I have said this before, but it bears repeating: Once every forty years I am naive enough to put my name on a down-and-out client's estate papers when they have no one else.

Beverly Creighton Read and the late George Allen had a lot in common.

I met Beverly Creighton Read, a.k.a. John Read, in about 2008. We both hung out at the lounge in the La Fonda Hotel in Santa Fe, New Mexico, for the country and western dancing. Our connection, in addition to having similar military backgrounds, turned out to be that Read's mentor and benefactor—back when he was a young lawyer with the Hunton & Williams law firm in Richmond, Virginia—was John E. McDonald. John was also a close friend of mine and a fellow Army Reserve JAG colonel. On occasions when McDonalds visited me in Santa Fe, we went out to dinner with Read and his current girlfriend—of which he had more of them than his share.

Read had gone on to be a prosecutor in Lexington, Virginia. He was a Vietnam veteran and had been severely wounded in battle. He was also a recovering alcoholic. He had been divorced and was estranged from his children and other family members. He was later disbarred for sexual misconduct, ethics violations, and prosecutorial misconduct by the Virginia Bar. He then moved to

Santa Fe New Mexico to start over. He had not spoken to his son in California in 30 years. I did have some limited contact with his daughter and a brother, but no family members came to visit during his memory decline.

He was a great dancer and a charmer. He lived with one woman, Debbie, for several years. He had a will leaving everything to her. Unfortunately, they broke up and she moved out, taking the original will with her. The way to revoke a will, if one does not have it to tear up or shred, is to make a new one. At his request I prepared a new will and drafted both a General Power of Attorney (POA) and a Medical POA. He had no one at the time and insisted on me being the personal representative in his will and to hold his POAs. I reluctantly agreed, assuming he would eventually get his life straightened out and this would all go away. Sound familiar?

He did not know whom he should designate to receive his estate now that Debbie was no longer living with him. I encouraged him to name his children as beneficiaries in the will, the normal resolution. It was lucky for John's kids that he had me to encourage him to do the right thing.

Lucky for former girlfriend Debbie, she still got a well-deserved $10,000 from a Veterans Administration (VA) insurance policy when he died. She had never been removed as the named beneficiary. I had not been made aware of any insurance policy until notified by the VA after his death.

Things rocked along fine for another couple of years until he began a descent into dementia, eventually becoming incompetent to make any decisions. I was now stuck with this assignment. The only other option would have been to get a guardian appointment with all the hassle and paperwork that entailed. A court would need to approve most activities and expenses. His situation became such that we had to place him in a string of dementia facilities in the Santa Fe area. He had to be moved to another facility occasionally because he was a difficult patient and was having sex with other dementia patients. Before we took away his cell phone, he even tried to arrange a marriage with another patient who was already married. I had to sell his now vacant house, which I was able to do with the POA, and place the money in his accounts.

One of his subsequent girlfriends, after Debbie, turned out to be a French expatriate, we lovingly called the French dip. My first recollection of her was when she appeared at a meeting with me, John, and one of his Veterans Administration doctors at his house. We were there to urge him to take his meds as prescribed. She insisted that John Read should have someone younger than me with his power of attorney. It was a slap at me. As best we could determine, she was out to get the money, but I was standing in the way. In his condition, he would tell her whatever she wanted to hear or promise her anything. After one of her periodic confrontations with me or Chavela Esparza, who had been his next-door neighbor for many years, or his caregivers, I told her, "You wanted his car; I sold the car. You wanted the house; I sold the house. The only thing he can give you now is herpes and genital warts." Not necessarily true, but it shut her up. Now she has another guy.

After we moved him to the first dementia facility, she would take him out dancing without my authorization or that of the nursing home. Sometimes she would keep him at her house for several days. In those situations, he sometimes got off his meds and ended up in the emergency room or else was found wandering along a city street. At about this same time, she showed up with him one evening at Tiny's, another country and western dance venue. In one of his rare lucid moments, he came over to me and said, "Peyton, I want to thank you for protecting my money from all those people trying to get it." She overheard his comment. After he had walked away, this classy girlfriend walked up, and in my face exhibited her middle finger.

Once she slipped a psychiatrist into one of the nursing homes after hours to examine him to prove him competent. If she could prove him competent, then he could leave all his estate to her with a new will. That too failed, as the shrink recognized Read's condition. Later, I had to shut down four consecutive law firms that she either contacted, or else had taken him to, to try to show him sufficiently competent to change his will and the powers of attorney, and to get me removed from both. Once I explained to these firms that I had a string of Veterans Administration physicians who will testify, correctly, that Read was incompetent to make any decisions at all, and if they wanted to go down that path, I would be the only one to make any money from their efforts, they immediately bowed out.

Lucky for me, I had delegated the medical responsibility under the medical POA to Chavela Esparza, the long-time next-door neighbor. She was used to dealing with the Veterans Administration on his behalf and had previously managed his bank accounts. The French gal gave her and the caregivers no end of grief. When Read died, she claimed that he wanted to be buried in Santa Fe rather than at the Arlington National Cemetery as detailed in his last will and testament. She insisted on seeing the body at the Funeral Home. She wanted to "kiss him goodbye." I reluctantly agreed to allow her despite protests from Chavela Esparza. When he was to be cremated, she followed the hearse from the funeral home to the cremation facility in Española. One strange lady.

Shortly before Read died, unknown to him due to his condition, he received a $185,000 IRA inheritance from the estate of an aunt. When I probated his estate in Santa Fe County, counting the IRA money, his total estate amounted to over $500,000. The IRA and other proceeds, after expenses, were divided between the son and daughter. We arranged for his ashes to be placed in Arlington National Cemetery in accordance with his wishes. I got paid adequately on this one.

John A. Rayburn

I have been for several years something like the unofficial general counsel of my Santa Fe country and western dance group. In this capacity I have frequently prepared free wills and powers of attorney for my dancing friends. We usually sign them at the bar at Tiny's or La Fonda. These are a couple of the dancing venues where it is easy to find a couple of disinterested witnesses. I also am a notary public which makes it easier to finalize the documents.

In March of 2022 I prepared a will and related estate documents for my friend John A. Rayburn. John taught concealed carry courses and dance classes at the Community College. He was a great dancer and would always dance with friends or guests we happened to have in town. I was unaware how sick he was at the time or much about his background outside of the dance or concealed carry crowd. He soon moved to Colorado where he lived with his companion Nancy Bono. He died there in December of 2022. His son, who lives in Silver Spring MD, was the beneficiary of the estate and the personal representative. We probated John's will in Santa Fe County and soon discovered that he had a vacant lot in Española that the city was trying to foreclose on for cleanup costs. There was a rush to get the probate process started to stop the foreclosure. Once we found a buyer for the lot, we discovered that his mother, who had died in 2001, was still on the deed. I had to do a quick probate in Rio Arriba County where she was living at death to clear the title. That county probate court got snowed in and we had several problems getting the paperwork to the title company in time. We did, and luckily. I got paid on the settlement sheet covering me for some fees and expenses of what was later to come.

It turns out that John was a real hoarder and never disposed of anything. Joe Juarez and one of my economic refugees Miguel and I cleaned out the house that he had rented on Agua Fria. We hauled sixteen pickup loads of trash, piled high, to the city dump. The place was a mess and there was even a pickup bed worth of ammunition, which is now in storage in the hopes of selling it. We then discovered that he owned two old airplanes, one a 2012 Luscombe and flyable based at the Santa Fe airport and a Piper Cub that was not flyable at the airport in Española. We had to sell both. One bank account in his name indicated that state retirement fund checks were being deposited monthly. There was about a $3000 balance left. When I inquired further as to the source, we discovered that his mother, a state employee who died in 2001, had retirement checks still going into John's account. Only in New Mexico would a state pension agency keep writing checks to a person who would be 112 years old at this point. In any event, they now want $187,000 refunded. This is probably not going to happen. John had not filed tax returns for over 10 years with the state of New Mexico or with the federal government.

Helmerich & Payne

I would often do legal work for Helmerich & Payne, a Fortune 500 contract oil and gas company in Tulsa, and was on a small retainer. They had several drilling rigs running in Venezuela at the time. I once got a call from the company at 3AM reporting they had an oil well fire on a rig on Lake Maracaibo in Venezuela. An American employee had been severely burned along with a Venezuelan employee. They had sent a plane from Tulsa to pick up the American. Upon arrival, they had a near revolt because the Venezuelan employees insisted that they put the injured Venezuelan worker on the plane. The plane departed for Tulsa with both, and my mission was to get clearance from the State Department on short notice so that the non-U.S. citizen could legally be brought to the burn unit in Tulsa.

Successes and Failures

I have had hundreds of successes, but a couple of failures come to mind from my sole practitioner days. These really were not my fault because people would not allow me to work on the problem to the end. Helmerich & Payne punched a 30,000-foot hole in the ground to discover natural gas in western Oklahoma. The location was on Indian lands, and a communalization agreement was required to be signed within a certain period. The deadline was missed due to the negligence of a staffer being out of the office taking a bar exam. Millions of dollars were at stake as I understand the process. I had been the counsel to American Indian National Bank and had met a number of Indian officials during the time of that bank's existence. One was a chief of an Oklahoma tribe who lived in Washington D.C. I mentioned the situation to him. He assured me that he personally knew the key folks at the Bureau of Indian Affairs office in Anadarko, Oklahoma, and that we could fix this problem.

I was working with the late Carl Young, assistant general counsel at H&P. The plan was that my Indian friend Carl and I would fly down to Anadarko on the little company Mitsubishi Two propeller plane and meet with the BIA officials and discretely resolve this mess. By the time the chief and I got to Tulsa, Walt Helmerich himself had gotten involved. He had called in Bill Paul, former head of the American Bar Association and a partner in a huge Oklahoma law firm, along with his assistants.

So instead of Carl, my Indian chief, and me flying down to Anadarko to quietly resolve this problem, we all flew down on the big H&P Jet. Of course, when we all walked into the BIA building with a now high-profile entourage, the government guys all came in on the other side of the table, and that effort promptly fell flat. Carl and I never got to follow our plan, which nine chances out of ten would have succeeded. Leon Gavras, the H&P General Counsel, passed it off with the comment: "We are a publicly held corporation, and when we get in trouble, we get the biggest law firm we can find, and even if they screw it up, we do not get in trouble with our shareholders." It still was a costly mistake.

A second one involved a former assistant director of the FBI, then a Vice President of large corporation. He had eight children. One of my responsibilities was to get the children jobs, and, if necessary, get them out of trouble. I got his older son a job with the National Labor Relations Board, as I was friends with the chairperson. He parlayed this experience into being a labor lawyer for Disney. Another son, who had been attending an Outward Bound program in New Mexico, boarded an American Airlines flight in Albuquerque. He had a climbing rope and a hook hanging over his shoulder. Even back before serious security he did stand out. A security person asked to see the ticket of the person that just got on the plane. It turned out that there was no ticket—as his sister, who was a flight attendant for American Airlines, was smuggling him on the plane to fly back to Washington. Former FBI agent charge in Albuquerque, Forest Putman, got the call from the dad's assistant to get the son out of jail. I got a call from the same assistant to go to the national airport and fix the problem on that end. I arrived about an hour and a half early and met with the head flight attendant supervisor. We chatted casually and drank coffee as we waited for the flight, winging its way from Albuquerque to D.C. I got her to admit that the daughter had not done anything that others had not done, and she was inclined to give her three days suspension. Unfortunately for the daughter, the dad could not leave it alone. He had to call Harvey Foster, former agent in charge the New York FBI office and then the head of security for American Airlines. Instantly, it became a high-profile labor management problem when the union representative walked into the room. The result was the daughter got fired.

I have been successful with fixing things when people leave me alone and do not interfere.

Pizza Hut

In 1981, in Carlisle Barracks, Pennsylvania, while on active duty completing the U.S. Army War College in 1981, I received a phone call from a former FBI agent friend, Hobson Adcock. He was an assistant to Cartha Deloach, a former assistant director of the FBI. Deloach at the time was Vice President for public affairs for PepsiCo Inc., then the parent company of Pepsi, Pizza Hut, Taco Bell, Frito Lay, and North American Van Lines. Hob related that one of their subsidiaries, Pizza Hut in Wichita, Kansas, had an issue before Congress concerning dairy price supports. He wanted to know if I were familiar with the program and if there was something I could do to help. The answer was yes.

Having grown up on a dairy farm and having been an aide to two different Secretaries of Agriculture, I had some general knowledge of the program. I promptly called a law school classmate friend still with the U.S. Department of Agriculture, Ted Bogan. Ted oversaw the Dairy Price Support Program with the Agriculture Stabilization and Conservation Service. Ted provided a quick update on the current issues. I then called Ed Brasa, an attorney in the PepsiCo Law Department at Pizza Hut in Wichita, Kansas. PepsiCo lawyers staffed the corporate law offices at all the subsidiaries. Ed came to Washington, D.C., and we attended some Congressional hearings on their issue and met with members of the Kansas Congressional delegation. Pizza Hut was the world's largest user of mozzarella cheese at the time. Shaving a penny a pound off the price of cheese translated into millions of dollars. The government support program, in effect, set the market price of cheese.

I worked on that issue for a few months with Ed Brasa until he moved to Taco Bell. He was succeeded by Lawrence (Larry) Schauf, also in the PepsiCo Law Department. Larry had testified at the Congressional hearings held by the Senate Agricultural Committee.

President Reagan signed one of our dairy price support bills in his hospital room (limiting our costs) after the attempted assassination to show the world that he was still functioning.

In early January 1983, I received an urgent call from Larry Whitt who had replaced Schauf at Pizza Hut when Schauf left to another company. January was a slow month for the pizza business. They wanted to do something to hype sales. Their outside marketing guru, Boris Weinstein in Pittsburg, Pennsylvania, had produced an idea to have a "National Pizza Week." They wanted me to get legislation through Congress to authorize this immediately.

After making the rounds on Capitol Hill with various contacts, I determined that to do what they wanted with legislation would take two or three years, if at all. Most Capitol Hill representatives and Senators hated commemoratives. I suggested another approach. I went to meet Secretary of Agriculture Richard Lyng, whom I knew well. I prevailed on him to sign a U.S. Department of Agriculture Proclamation declaring a Pizza Week without the "National" designation, which was reserved for Congress. In their national advertising, Pizza Hut could call it National Pizza Week or State Pizza Week, or anything they wanted. I had given them a hook for their advertising campaign. Pizza Week, the second week in January, is still alive and well 30 years later.

I was skiing in Aspen a couple of weeks later with friends from Tulsa. While there, I caught a TV news program showing reporters interviewing people on the street in New York City and asking them how they felt about National Pizza Week. Chalk up another success. A year or so ago I was in St. Louis and the restaurants there were still advertising Pizza Week.

Other major Pizza Hut lobbying successes included getting Pizza Hut into the school lunch program and fixing a FICA tax issue for delivery drivers worth millions. I made the Wall Street Journal on that one. The article referred to me as a high-powered PepsiCo lobbyist and authored by WSJ reporter Glenn Simpson, later of Fusion GPS fame in the impeachment effort toward President Trump.

Pizza Hut had developed a new menu dish they called "Preatso." The commercial for this new product needed to be filmed in Italy to give it credibility, and they wanted to use authentic U.S. food products. They immediately ran into a problem in that Italy limited entry of U.S. meat products. To get around this, on one day's notice, I had the American Embassy's agricultural attaché in Rome meet the plane and escort the needed U.S. meat products to the location for the commercial to get around the Italian government's restrictions.

Pizza Hut was also a large user of canned mushrooms. The domestic producers and the Taiwanese producers ganged up on the People's Republic of China (PRC), which was where Pizza Hut got most of their mushrooms. This precipitated a hearing at the International Trade Commission in Washington D.C. The official in charge of anything bottled or canned in the PRC came to D.C. for this hearing. The evening before, I picked him up at the Chinese Embassy for a dinner at a top Chinese restaurant. He wore his Nehru jacket and was accompanied by two aides who looked like Harvard MBAs in regular suits and ties. They spoke fluent English and he did not. During dinner, he would place items on my plate with his chopsticks and insist I try them. It was a fascinating evening with his aides as translators.

I learned a lot about mushrooms. For many years domestic canned mushrooms frequently resulted in food poisoning or recalls. PRC canning methods are primitive. They put sufficient heat in the canning process, though, and they have no such food safety problems. They claim they can the best part of the mushrooms. Domestic producers' fresh mushrooms usually go to salad bars, while the stems and pieces are canned. I am reminded of the "mushroom theory of management" and have at times been the victim. Mushrooms are reportedly kept in the dark with manure thrown on them.

Wendy's

Larry Schauf had been at Pizza Hut but later was General Counsel at Wendy's. Wherever he went, he usually took me with him. I became the lawyer and lobbyist for Wendy's Corporation and kept PepsiCo's Pizza Hut as a client. Most of the Wendy's issues involved meat inspection, food safety, and employer-mandated regulations.

The Wendy's founder, Dave Thomas, was pretty much out of running the company at the time I became involved. He came to Washington on adoption policy matters for meetings with Senators and Congressmen on occasion. We would then use him on Capitol Hill for lobbying on company issues. Dave had been adopted as an infant. A brief time later his adoptive mother died. He bounced around the country with his ne'er do well adoptive father. Eventually, as a teenager, he dropped out and lived in the YMCA in Indianapolis, Indiana. There he worked in restaurants. He was drafted into the Army, where he ran noncommissioned officer (NCO) clubs. After the Army stint, he ended up an aide or driver for Colonel Sanders of Kentucky Fried Chicken. After a few years there, Colonel Harlan Sanders let him take over four troubled KFC restaurants. From there, he made his first million and then started his own restaurant chain.

After doing his own commercials, Dave became quite a celebrity. He would be mobbed by tourists in the halls of Congress when I escorted him around Capitol Hill. I could always get an appointment with almost any Senator or Congressman. They wanted to meet him, and their staff members wanted to meet him. What those who knew Dave only from television did not know was that those commercials took lots of takes to get Dave to come across as warm and fuzzy. He was just a gruff old guy who knew how to run restaurants.

His passion, though, was adoption policy. He knew that his own adoption had been a disaster, but he thought he was 100 percent better off than all the kids stuck in foster care. He therefore established the Dave Thomas Foundation for Adoption. The money from his books and golf tournaments went to the foundation. Our lobbying efforts for the foundation were intended to make it easier, via tax incentives, for companies to provide adoption benefits with their employee health and benefit plans. He gave me a "Dave Thomas Big Bertha" golf club.

He became a celebrity from his commercials and was becoming a role model for kids. He had never finished high school, so in his sixties while living in Florida he decided to get his GED. The high school class graduating that year adopted him with their class. He was reportedly voted the most likely to succeed. He was prom king, and his wife was prom queen.

Senate Honorariums

In the 1970s, honorariums were payments made to Senators for making appearances or speeches. These were nice opportunities for lobbyists to gain access and were often sought after by the Senators or Congressmen themselves. They could pick up a quick $2,000 for a 30-minute talk to some business group or convention or at a company headquarters. Later, after a lot of bad publicity, they still received the honorariums, but they donated them to charity. As far as I know, they can no longer receive them at all.

Over a period of several years, I arranged for Senators such as Bob Dole, David Boren, David Pryor, Don Nichols, et al, to speak at PepsiCo headquarters in Purchase, New York, where I got to meet Don Kendall, and to AIG headquarters on Wall Street in New York, where I got to meet Maurice Greenberg. It was beneficial to me as I got to fly on the New York shuttle with a Senator and to have a captive audience of two or three hours of travel time to advance my client's issues.

Once we needed Bob Dole to speak at an event in

California for Pizza Hut, which at the time was head-quartered in his state of Kansas. We lined up a string of honorariums at other companies in the area. He could pick up a pot of money in a brief time on one trip. By doing so, it was insurance that he would not likely cancel out on us at the last minute.

One Acre Mineral Interest Split Fifteen Ways

My first quiet title case in New Mexico involved a one-acre mineral interest in Lea County. My grandfather T.H. George in Ada, Oklahoma acquired a one-acre mineral interest in 1929. We have no idea how that happened, maybe he won it in a poker game. In any event, no one knew about it until oil was struck in the section of land in which the interest was located, and the lease hounds or brokers started trying to chase down hares. Rather than trying to probate a half a dozen estates in New Mexico for my grandparents, I filed a quiet title action with a notarized complaint swearing to the facts I set forth as to percentages of interests in those fifteen of us living. I then had all the siblings, cousins, nephews, etc., who descended from my grandfather file answers swearing to the facts in my complaint so there were no facts in dispute. Computations were complicated be-cause some my grandfather's children had five kids, and some had three or none. I had a Zoom conference with the judge during the pandemic. She instructed me to publish a notice against unknown heirs. I did, and now we all get small checks.

Family

Nancy Whorton George

I met my wife of 36 years, Nancy Lou Whorton, on a blind date in Ada, Oklahoma, in 1963. I had been an FBI Agent for a year and had returned to Oklahoma on vacation. Nancy had grown up in Haywood and Arpelar, Oklahoma, in Pittsburg County near McAlister. Her father had a ranch and two country grocery stores and gas stations. As a barefoot kid, she pumped gas and talked to everyone. In later years, her outgoing personality from her childhood days made her just as comfortable talking to heads of major corporations and political elites as with anyone else. She was attending East Central State College in Ada when we met, but transferred later to University of Oklahoma, where she graduated. Our date was arranged by her college roommate and our mutual friend Molly Shi. Molly was later married to one of my oil field worker friends, Gerald Ford, before marrying Dave Boren, who at the time was Governor of Oklahoma and later a Senator. Nancy and I were attracted to each other instantly and engaged briefly. That broke off, but we stayed connected.

After Nancy graduated from the University of Oklahoma, she went to New York City to work for Lanvin Ritz Cosmetics in Public Relations. There she was involved in a program called Miss Ritz, marketing high-end cosmetics on college campuses. I was an FBI agent in the Newark, New Jersey, FBI office at the time. We saw one another frequently. After I was transferred to the Atlantic City FBI Resident Agency, she came down occasionally on weekends.

Shortly after I was transferred to Washington, D.C., she left her glamor job in New York and moved to D.C. She taught school in Prince Georges County, Maryland, for a couple of years. We were married in 1966 in Ada, Oklahoma. She worked for the American Home Economics Association and later in the University of Oklahoma's Washington office. She even taught Wendy Ward Charm School for little girls. After I completed law school, she finished law school and was admitted to the D.C. bar. We then practiced law together for a brief period.

She and I worked on Multi-Employer Pension Plan Act Amendments (MPPAA) legislation for Frito Lay, a PepsiCo subsidiary. Nancy would go to Capitol Hill and make the contacts with members of Congress and come back and tell me how it went. I would then report our progress to Roger King, Vice President at Frito Lay at the time. One day I got everything completely screwed up in repeating her report. She grabbed the phone and started talking directly to Roger. She was off and running. She was instrumental in saving the company over four million dollars by getting an amendment that exempted them. Her main supporter in that effort, Senator David Boren, the previous Governor of Oklahoma, even shut down the Senate until her provision was included in the overall legislation.

Roger moved on to Vice President for personnel at PepsiCo and would later be her coach when El Paso Energy was trying to hire her as a Vice President. We both worked on a coal slurry pipeline legislation issue for Ken

Lay when he was at Florida Gas. He became another big client for her over the subsequent years. In 1975 I was recruited to open a D.C. office for Miles and Stockbridge, a large Baltimore Law firm, and Nancy went out on her own, moving to a lobbying office near Capitol Hill.

Nancy and the Secretary of Energy

Jim Edwards was a dentist by training but had been the governor of South Carolina. He was appointed the Secretary of Energy during the Reagan administration. When he and his wife, Ann, came to Washington, the Boren's, with whom they had been friends as former governors, had planned to help them find a house. However, at the time of their move, Senator David Boren and wife Molly were unavailable. They asked Nancy to find a place for the Edwards. She found them a house to rent, and we loaned them an extra washer and dryer we had. We stayed connected with them socially.

Several months after Edwards became Secretary of Energy, Nancy was standing in line waiting for a Senate committee hearing. She struck up a conversation with a fellow standing in line with her, Malcolm Hood. He was a lobbyist for the Louisiana Interstate Gas Corporation (LIG). During the hour or so that they had to wait before the doors were opened, they chatted. He told her some of the issues that they were concerned about and suggested that his company really needed someone like her in Washington. A few weeks later, he brought his boss, Jim Terrill, President of LIG, to D.C. for some meetings and to meet Nancy. She had since learned more about the issues which they were particularly concerned about.

The three had breakfast so she could meet Terrill. During the breakfast she told them that she had scheduled a meeting with the Secretary of Energy for them at 10AM. Terrill pooh-poohed the whole idea, insisting that the issue they were concerned about was so hot that the Secretary of Energy was refusing to meet with any of the pipeline companies. Nancy told him to do what he liked, but that she and Malcolm were going to meet with Secretary Edwards.

When they arrived at the secretary's office at 10AM, Jim Terrill was already waiting for them, pacing the floor. Secretary Edwards came out of his office and gave Nancy a big hug. He introduced himself to Jim Terrill and Malcolm Hood and proceeded to congratulate them on having "the best energy lobbyist in Washington." "She even has the key to my house, and I'm using her washer and dryer," he added.

Edwards allowed Terrill 30 minutes to make all his points. Once they walked out of the Secretary's office, Terrill turned to Nancy and said, "Where can we go for lunch? We want to retain you." That is when she picked up her very own pipeline client. We had crawfish boils in our back yard for Congressional staff, and we got to New Orleans frequently while she represented LIG, an intrastate pipeline in Louisiana.

Transco Pipeline Company

Nancy represented Transco in several tax matters. She was able to get major legislation through Congress allowing master limited partnerships now utilized by many large companies for tax benefits. Transco had a corporate apartment in the Waldorf Towers at the Waldorf Hotel in New York City. Nancy had access as needed and periodically took some of the women legislative staff on the Finance and Ways and Means Committees to New York City for shopping trips. She was part of the original group of women lobbyists and Congressional staff that formed the Women's Tax Coalition. This was a time when women were just moving into key staff positions on Capitol Hill. While recovering from breast cancer later, her support system of gals on the tax writing committees kept moving her legislative matters forward even though she was at home.

President Reagan appointed Nancy to the 10-person Advisory Committee on Federal Assistance for Alternative (Clean Energy) Fuels Demonstration Facilities, a position she held from 1982 to 1987, and Secretary of Energy Jim Edwards appointed her to the National Advisory Board for Conservation and Extension Service. She served on that board from 1988 to 1992.

From Houston Natural Gas to Internorth to Enron

Nancy had worked directly on legislative matters for Ken Lay at Florida Gas, and when he moved to Houston Natural Gas, she continued as a lobbyist for his new company. Houston National Gas merged with Internorth, another large pipeline company, and their headquarters got moved to Omaha, Nebraska. Houston Natural Gas had a subsidiary, Belco. When one of their oil production platforms off the coast of Peru was appropriated by that government, Nancy came up with a plan allowing a better tax write-off for the company. Senator Zorinsky of Nebraska was her lead sponsor in the Senate, supporting the interests of a Nebraska company. She got her favorable tax provision out of the Senate just as the Houston Natural Gas boys took over Internorth. They immediately moved the headquarters to Houston, effectively pulling the rug from under Senator Zorinsky, her sponsor. Nancy had worked on this issue for a couple of years and had been well compensated all along by the client.

She received a call from Ken Lay to come to Houston. She was not sure what that was about but waited outside a board meeting for about three hours before Lay emerged. Lay apologized for having to pull the rug out from under her and the Senator. He explained that for other reasons they had to move the headquarters out of Omaha. He handed her a check for $50,000. She is the only lobbyist I know who ever got a bonus for losing.

911 Call from a Hospital Room

Nancy was diagnosed with breast cancer in 1991 and was treated at Georgetown University Hospital. Part of her treatment involved having a mastectomy. Unfortunately, at the time of her surgery the hospital was full, and it was a holiday weekend. After the surgery, they moved her to recover in a ward that was really for the terminally ill instead of being for patients who were recovering from surgery. They had temporary staff on duty in this ward.

During the several weeks of the ordeal of her treatment, I was trying to run both my law firm and her lobbying efforts. I had been at the hospital until about 10PM that night after her surgery and had finally gone home. I was exhausted. Shortly after I had left the hospital, she realized that she was bleeding from the surgery. She kept ringing the buzzer, and the nurse would come in and just try to console her as if she were dying but did nothing. She then called me at home. While I was trying to get through to Georgetown Hospital officials, she called 911 from her hospital bed to tell the police dispatcher that she was bleeding to death. She got some vital and immediate attention as a furious team of doctors came running into her ward yelling at her for calling 911. She had it all recorded at the police department though. Once they checked her condition, they realized that she was in fact bleeding out, and had saved her own life.

She was the only person I have known who dialed 911 from a hospital bed.

Red Jaguar

Because Nancy represented several of their major competitors, El Paso Natural Gas wanted to hire her to come in house, be a Vice President, and run their Washington office. This involved their lobbying and regulatory affairs. She had just gone through breast cancer with surgery and chemo. She was not sure she even wanted another job. At El Paso they thought she was negotiating. Their CEO Bill Wise kept raising the ante, and she finally became interested. She was being coached by her old client, Roger King, Vice President of personnel for PepsiCo. He would tell her what to ask for and what to ignore "because everybody got it." She cut a great deal with stock options, perks, and benefits. The CEO told her he would provide her with a car. She told him she had a car. He told her he would get her any car she wanted. She told him she wanted a Red Jaguar. That sealed the deal. Her company car with El Paso was a red Jaguar Vanden Plas. The next year they gave company cars to the corporate officers and imputed the value as income to them. It was a joyful day for her when they moved the headquarters to Houston from El Paso. She had to fly there every couple of weeks, and Houston was much less of a hassle.

"Run for it!"

El Paso Energy, now Kinder Morgan, was having a customer meeting in Amelia Island, Florida. Unfortunately, it fell over Mother's Day Weekend. Nancy was tasked to get a big-name speaker for the event, preferably a Senator. The only Senator she could prevail on to do this for her was Senator John Breau of Louisiana. He would be giving up a weekend with his wife and two daughters. His condition was that he be flown down on one of the company jets, go a couple of days early so he could have a day with the tennis pro and a day with the golf pro at the Ritz Carlton Resort where the event was being held.

The three of us flew down on one of El Paso's corporate jets. On the evening before the meeting started, we took a shuttle from the hotel to a nice restaurant in the town of Amelia Island. We enjoyed a great dinner and a couple of bottles of wine. Just as we finished dinner, it was starting to rain. We saw out the window that the hotel shuttle was pulling up. Nancy told the Senator and me to run to catch and hold the shuttle while she paid the check. It turned out that she left with the original signed copy of an excessively big American Express bill and instead left the unsigned copy on the table. By the time we got back to the hotel, everyone was trying to find her to get this straightened out.

The next morning at the meeting of their customers from the southeastern part of the U.S., the Senator began his presentation by telling the customers what a wonderful company El Paso was. He told them that he knew how the company was making so much money. He said they take you to great restaurants, they ply you with mighty fine wine and great food, but when the bill comes, they say, "Run for it!" My wife could have killed him, but everybody, including her CEO, got a laugh out of it at her expense.

Governor Richardson

My first visit to Santa Fe, New Mexico, was in 1972. I was in Albuquerque, New Mexico, preparing an event for Secretary of Agriculture Earl Butz, and his bodyguard Jack Neese and I had a free afternoon. Since the Forest Service is part of the USDA Jack and I misappropriated a U.S. Forest Service car and drove it up to Santa Fe just to see what it looked like. I never dreamed at the time that I would later live there.

When Nancy became a Vice President of El Paso Energy, the head of their trade association told her that she needed to work on Congressman Bill Richardson. He was on the House Interstate and Foreign Commerce Committee. El Paso was one of the largest taxpayers in the State of New Mexico. And work on him we did to acquaint him with her company interests.

We would take him and his entire staff periodically to the Red Sage Restaurant for dinner even though most lobbyists just dealt with the administrative or legislative assistant. Nancy and I were in New Orleans shortly after our several dinners at the Red Sage. We were there for an event involving Louisiana Interstate Gas (LIG), one of

Nancy's clients, when she received a call from Congressman Richardson. He was receiving the Aztec Eagle Award from President Carlos Salinas in Mexico City. This is the highest award that a non-Mexican citizen could receive. He invited Nancy to join him for the ceremony at the Mexican White House. She could not very well say no because of the company's position in New Mexico. She assumed, however, that there would be every energy lobbyist in Washington there for this ceremony. Upon arrival at the Mexican White House, Los Pintos, she found that his entourage consisted of his wife, his mother, one other person, and Nancy. Whatever we had been doing was working.

When we came to New Mexico we were on the opposite side of Richardson politically, and we stayed away to avoid being drawn into fundraisers. We did see Richardson and his wife occasionally in Santa Fe restaurants.

Nancy ended up in hospice for the last two months of her life. Betsy Mohler was a dear friend of Nancy's. She had been on the staff of the Senate Energy Committee and was later the Chairman of the Federal Energy Regulatory Commission (FERC) before serving as Deputy Secretary of Energy under Bill Richardson. Betsy came out to visit Nancy during Christmas week in 2002. While in Santa Fe she said she would like to see Governor-Elect Bill Richardson. I took her down to the Roundhouse, the state capitol. This was three days before he was to be sworn in as governor. I had never been to the Roundhouse before. There was no security like we were used to in D.C. Betsy, and I wandered around on the ground floor and finally found a janitor whom we asked where we might find Bill Richardson. He told us that his secret office was in Room 400, but he was in a meeting in Room 300 right then. We were used to Washington D.C. security in government buildings, where you are almost patted down. In contrast there was no security there in the Roundhouse.

When we got to the correct floor, Richardson was in a meeting in a conference room. He saw Betsy and me outside the door. He came out, gave her a hug, and shook hands with me. She explained that she was there because Nancy was in hospice. He called Nancy a couple of days later and told her he planned to visit her, but she died a couple of weeks into his term before he could do so. Ken Lay called her in middle of all his legal difficulties, including the collapse of Enron and the criminal charges, and they talked a long time. She was able to thank him for all he did for her.

In 2011 I happened to be at a dinner party in Santa Fe at Gerald Peters' home with my son and his wife and my companion Barbara. Governor Bill Richardson, who would be leaving office in six days, was also there. He had just returned from North Korea for a diplomatic mission. I went over and introduced myself. I told him my late wife was Nancy George with El Paso Energy. He lit up like a Christmas tree, came over and told my son how his mom taught him everything he knew about energy. He talked with Barbara about her prominent New Mexico families, the Catron's, Luna's and Bergère's. He told us of his effort to back the North Koreans down from their threats. He then turned to me full face and said, "Peyton: is there anything I can do for you in my last six days as governor?" That is not the way things usually happen, but I did not have anybody I needed a pardon for. I told him he needed to fix lawyer reciprocity, which at the time was not permitted in New Mexico, because New Mexico is always going to be on the top of the bad lists and at the bottom of the good lists in this area until this issue is fixed. He replied, "Oh?" He had no clue what I was talking about, and it is really a New Mexico Supreme Court issue, but the former Governor could owe me one.

Santa Fe and Saying Goodbye

We would visit Santa Fe several times a year. El Paso was a big sponsor of the Santa Fe Opera at the time. Nancy would bring Congressional groups out to tour the gas processing facilities in Farmington and wine and dine them in Santa Fe. Sometimes I would go along and sometimes not. El Paso Energy happened to be one of the largest taxpayers in New Mexico.

For the Santa Fe Opera opening night, the CEO would have his tailgate party tent on the grounds with the board of directors as his guests. Nancy was usually delegated to entertain Governor Gary Johnson. Each year Nancy and I would bring two couples from D.C. as our guests. Our El Paso group would take over the Inn of the Anasazi, a charming hotel in downtown Santa Fe. Stretch limos would be brought in from Las Vegas to take our guests around. Our guests were usually Nancy's contemporaries who also ran Washington offices of major corporations. With the opera and the events they hosted, they certainly spent more money than the fast food restaurant chains I represented.

Nancy was fascinated with Santa Fe. She was interested in the arts, and Santa Fe was touted as the third largest art capital in the world. She really wanted to retire to Santa Fe. Each time we went there, we would look for houses. We agreed that we wanted something close to the city center that was not on a dirt road. We eventually bought a property at 907 Santa Fe Trail, three blocks from the state capitol. We did a complete renovation and finally moved there in November 2001.

Two months after we moved in, Nancy was tired all the time. We attributed this to having Christmas guests and from all the rigors of moving in. Her illness manifested itself with nosebleeds. In hindsight, she had all the symptoms; we just did not know what they were symptoms of. She went to one Santa Fe ear, nose, and throat doctor. He told her the problem was Santa Fe dry air and to get over it. He cauterized one side of her nose. She was still growing more tired by the day. She went back a week later to his partner, who cauterized the other side of her nose.

A nurse in that office realized that this was not really working. She pulled Nancy aside and suggested she go to a walk-in clinic off Rodeo Road in Santa Fe. The doctor there told her that it was a virus, and it would go away, but gave her a Zithromax pack for bacteria, which I thought a little strange.

We had been scheduled to do a ski trip in Aspen with some of her friends from D.C. She insisted that I go without her. I thought at the time she would be over this any day and suggested she might as well feel bad in Aspen rather than feel bad in Santa Fe. I went on the trip alone, but two days into the trip I got a call and she said, "I'm really sick; please come home." I hopped in my Jeep and drove back that night.

The following morning, I got on the phone to Mayo Clinic in Scottsdale, Arizona. We had planned eventually to get annual physicals there. I told the receptionist that my wife was not feeling well, and we would like to get the physical exams sooner rather than later. She booked us in three days. We took the motor home, towing the Jeep, to Scottsdale. By this time, she was so weak she had to hang on to my arm to walk. We still assumed that she would be well any day, due to what the Santa Fe doctors had told us. We thought we would visit some friends in Arizona and knock around there for a couple of weeks.

The luck of the draw for the annual physical for Nancy happened to be Connie Mariano, a retired Navy admiral. She had been the White House physician for presidents George Bush and Bill Clinton. Within two hours of doing lab tests and making other appointments, we were paged by Dr. Mariano. She told me that she had a team of doctors waiting for Nancy at the Mayo Clinic Hospital several miles away, and to get her there immediately. The doctors told her she would be dead in two weeks if not treated. They gave her multiple blood transfusions and diagnosed her with acute leukemia, which a high-school biology student probably could have determined.

I spent the next few weeks living in the motor home in the Mayo Hospital parking lot. Nancy had round after round of chemo. This involved being in a hospital about five days, then being out of the hospital about ten days, staying in Phoenix. She could come back to New Mexico for a couple of weeks, then turn around and do it all over again. She had thirty-eight blood transfusions that year.

The original diagnosis was in mid-January of 2002. By September, the Mayo doctors thought that they had gotten a leg up on it. When she first was admitted to Mayo, we had informed her friends, David and Molly

Boren in Oklahoma, of her hospitalization. (David was then the President of the University of Oklahoma.) At the time of my call, they were having dinner with Henry Zarrow, a mega-millionaire oil-field pipe supply company owner in Tulsa. In the lobby of Mayo Hospitals there are numerous plaques listing the Zarrow Foundation as a major benefactor.

The three of them got on the phone to Dr. Dave Utes, who was previously the chief of staff at Mayo in Rochester. He was the grand old man of urology and had treated Senators David Boren and Don Nickles, as well as President Ronald Reagan. Utes had just retired to Scottsdale. He would come in to visit Nancy and check on her. The Mayo doctors assured her that they had a conference call every morning on her case with Rochester. I presume she got the best possible care.

Unfortunately, when she went back in November 2002, even after all the chemo, the leukemia had come back. The doctors told her that they could send her to MD Anderson for some very experimental treatment but that she would die in the hospital. They claimed that the leukemia had been caused by chemo for breast cancer twelve years earlier. The chemo somehow started a reaction in the bone marrow in some patients that eventually became acute leukemia.

Nancy died on January 26, 2003, in hospice in Santa Fe, New Mexico. We had a memorial service for her at the President's House at the University of Oklahoma, sponsored by David and Molly Boren, and a memorial service in Alexandria, Virginia, put on by her D.C. area friends. She was cremated in Santa Fe, and we placed her ashes in Arlington National Cemetery. She was eligible because of my military service.

We were not sure the ashes would arrive in time, but they did on a cold snowy February day. My son Richard, a friend from the Pentagon Andy Lawrence, and I, along with an Army chaplain, walked into the waiting room at Arlington National Cemetery. There waiting for us was my old company commander, the Four-Star General Richard H. Thompson and his wife Pat. Pat volunteered there and had seen Nancy's name on the list of those being interred. This made it even more special. Thompson, as captain, had been my CO at Fort Chaffee in 1957 for basic training when I was a Private E-1. I worked directly for him 30 years later as a colonel when he was a four-star general. He and his wife loved Nancy. The general saw me as some kid off the farm that he had motivated and who had turned out okay. They used to invite us to parties at their quarters at Fort McNair.

I have such gratitude for the thirty-six great years Nancy and I had together, and for the son we raised together. She was one of a kind and a real go-getter. We were quite a power couple.

Barbara Bergère Nau

When my wife Nancy and I left Santa Fe in my Bluebird Wander lodge RV for the Mayo Clinic in Arizona, and before Nancy's diagnosis of leukemia, my then 92-year-old neighbor, Richard Lang, saw us as we were leaving. He told us, "When you come back here, don't back her in there too tight. I want to go somewhere in that."

A few months later I was back in Santa Fe with the motor home. I needed to take it down to a Cummins Diesel place in Albuquerque for service. I asked Richard if he wanted to go along with me, which of course he did. Richard had been an old horse soldier in the cavalry in the 1930s and claimed to have trained the first woman cavalry unit at the request of Eleanor Roosevelt. A colorful guy, he had been the head of Selective Service in New Mexico during the Eisenhower administration.

Lang rented a guest house a half-block down the street from my residence. The main house had been sold three times in forty-three years, but Richard, the tenant, always went with the deal. During the construction and renovation of my property, he was at my house nearly every day, watching the construction, and talking to the workers in Spanish or English.

He was more than happy to go for the ride. Once we got to Albuquerque, I dropped the motorhome off for repairs and unhooked the Jeep, my tow vehicle. I had several errands to run in Albuquerque. Richard had not been down to Albuquerque in many months, and he had a list of his own. He pulled out a piece of paper that had a phone number. He asked that I call this number and see if a lady was still in the hospital. I called the number, and sure enough, seventy year-old Barbara Bergère Nau, Santa Fe High class of 1956, was there for a hip replacement. She had lost her husband to cancer several years earlier.

It was her first day after surgery for a hip replacement. We met her daughter and other family members who were in her hospital room. Richard Lang had been her mother's boyfriend from 1955, when her dad had died, until 1975, when her mother died. He was like a grandfather to her daughter. Barbara would come up to Santa Fe to check on him periodically and to see that he got his medications. If I were in Santa Fe, they might call me to join them for lunch. When in Albuquerque I might join them for lunch with the Association of Foreign Intelligence Officers, an organization Richard belonged to, as he had been in the Counter-Intelligence Corps and OSS during World War II.

Barbara was on a list of the people that I kept informed on Nancy's progress with her medical issues. After Nancy died, I had gone back to D.C. for a while for the memorial service and to see my son and his family. When I returned to New Mexico, I received an email from Barbara suggesting that if I ever got down to Albuquerque to give her a call, and that she would be happy to buy me a cup of coffee. This was probably the most brazen thing she had ever done. That was the beginning of twelve great years with a great lady I would never have known but for Richard Lang.

I did have an opportunity to get to Albuquerque a few weeks later. Once there I discovered that the former FBI Agent breakfast I was planning to attend had been canceled. I gave Barbara a call. She was still working then for an aerospace company as an administrative assistant. We met for coffee. Our coffee date turned into lunch, and she came up to Santa Fe for brunch the following weekend.

A few weeks later, I told her I had left my motor home in Oklahoma where I had attended a memorial service before flying on to D.C. I needed to go pick it up and visit some friends and family. I suggested that she meet me in Dallas. I wanted to go to an RV rally in Tucson, Arizona. A real risk taker, she signed on to this, thinking at the time that an RV was a pop-up camper on the back of pickup.

She flew to Dallas's Love Field; how appropriate! We went to Mansion at Turtle Creek for dinner. I had parked the bus at an RV resort out west of Fort Worth, so I could make it to El Paso the first day. When we arrived, she was looking around for the pop-up camper on the pickup. My luxury RV had three air conditioners and a washer and dryer. She decided maybe she could live with that for a while.

Along the way from Fort Worth to El Paso, she kept getting calls from lady friends asking if they needed to call 911. They thought she was crazy going off with this guy she had been spending time together with for a week or two. We were laughing our heads off. We stopped in Midland, Texas, at some George-Bush-favorite barbecue place, according to their signs. Mid-afternoon, we were on Interstate 10 between Midland and El Paso in the middle of nowhere. I was getting tired, so I told her it was her turn to drive. I pulled over, and she drove while I took a nap. We made it to El Paso that night and had dinner with one of my scout-car partners from the Oklahoma City Police Department, Mel Kiesel. Several of the guys at OCPD who got in trouble or crossways with the Chief in the early sixties ended up on the El Paso PD at the time. We made it on to Tucson the following day.

We joined a rally with twenty-five other Bluebird motorhomes. We spent four days with these mostly small business guys and gals from all over the United States and had a wonderful time. From there, we went to Phoenix, where I parked the motorhome and stayed in the Sanctuary Resort while I got my annual physical at the Mayo Clinic. We then returned to Santa Fe in the RV and had fifty people in for cocktails that weekend.

Barbara grew up in Santa Fe and went to Santa Fe High School. She went away to college and never came back, although she and her husband later lived in Albuquerque. She claimed she never wanted to come back to Santa Fe, because both sides of the family were prominent, and it was like living in a fishbowl. I reintroduced her to her hometown and her very prominent family there.

Her great grandfather, Thomas B. Catron, was the first Senator from New Mexico, and at one time reportedly owned all the land from Santa Fe to Colorado but could not hang on to it because of the taxes. There was still a Catron Law Firm, occupied by a couple of her cousins, one who founded the Santa Fe Opera. Her mother was a Catron. Catron is the first of three counties named after the family.

Her grandfather on her father's side of the family, Alfred Bergère, came to the U.S. from Liverpool, England, in the 1880s. He was trained as a concert pianist in Liverpool. His mother had died, and his father gave him some money and a trunk full of clothes and put him on a boat to live with relatives in New York. He reportedly played at Carnegie Hall, but when the railroads were finished, he came to New Mexico as a peddler selling mining supplies to miners. His last name was Berger in Europe, and he Jewish, but when he came to New Mexico he added an "e," so everyone thought he was French, then he became a Catholic.

Alfred was friends with Manuel Otero, who was subsequently killed in a gunfight. Alfred Bergère married his widow, Alois Luna Otero, who had grown up in Luna Mansion in Los Lunas, New Mexico. The Luna family had a 65,000-acre sheep ranch from a Spanish land grant. The Berger family home is now the Georgia O'Keeffe Foundation house on Grant Street in Santa Fe. Barbara's father was born in that house, the youngest of fifteen kids.

Returning from one of our European trips in 2010, Barbara was diagnosed with lung cancer and had a lobe removed. A year later, the cancer had metastasized to her spine and elsewhere. She survived on a drug called Tarceva, which targeted the protein in the cancer cell. It eventually wore off, and we spent six months trying to get her into a clinical trial in Denver. By the time I got her into the trial, she was too weak to benefit from it. They released her after three weeks, and she died three weeks later. Barbara was one of the nicest, sweetest people I have ever known. She and I had twelve great years together and traveled the world.

Number One Daughter Vicky

Many of these situations do not have a happy conclusion, but this one certainly has. When people ask me how many children I have, my reply anymore is, "Two that I know about."

Mike Mapp is a rancher and builder in Ada, Oklahoma. He and his wife Vicky have a large ranch near Ada. Vicky was a Vice President for information technology at Prepaid Legal, Now Legal shield, a publicly held legal insurance company. She was fifty-three in 2012.

Mike told my brother, Lee George, also a rancher who lives on the place where we grew up, that Vicky's late mother, on her death bed, told Vicky that the guy she thought was her father was not, and that I was her father. My brother told me, and I thought, "Hmm, that's interesting."

I had a law enforcement friend in California pull her Oklahoma driver's license to determine when she was born. That way I could determine where I was some nine months earlier. It turns out that I had had a brief fling with her mother. This was back in my oil field days. It was still a major surprise to me, though. Happily, Vicky was a successful corporate officer of a publicly held company instead of some pole dancer on meth I probably deserved.

I began to follow her on the Prepaid Legal website. Her sixth-grade teacher had been in my high school class. She and I were friends on Facebook. Occasionally, the names of people we each may know pop up on Facebook. One day, Vicky's name popped up, and I clicked on it. She came right back with a message that if I ever came back to Oklahoma, she would look forward to visiting with me. At that point, she knew who I was, and I knew who she was. We began exchanging emails. In my first email, my first question was what was on her birth certificate. It was not me. My second question was when did she realize that she was more intelligent and better looking (smile)?

Barbara Nau and I got to Ada, Oklahoma, a few months later. Vicky walked into a restaurant to meet us with her husband and son. It was just surreal. She looked very much like my younger sister Jodie. Barbara and I were staying at a motel in Ada where we hosted a reception for some of my friends still there and some of Vicky's friends. Barbara bought me a box of cigars that read, "It's a girl," which I passed out. Shortly thereafter, my sister hosted a reception for us in Oklahoma City. A few weeks later, I took Vicky and her family, my son Richard and his family, and Barbara's daughter and family to Bermuda for a week. I thought they should get acquainted.

Vicky and I did a DNA test, not that I needed it, but she was my then 95-year-old mother's oldest grandchild, and I did not want other family members pushing back on her. The DNA test result came back at 99.99% with the caption, "We cannot eliminate this person as the father of this child." We then set out to correct her birth certificate. We sent in an affidavit along with the DNA test results to the State of Oklahoma Bureau of Vital Statistics. The Agency promptly kicked it back with their response indicating that since her mother was dead, we would need a court order.

I filed a suit in Pontotoc County, Oklahoma, to establish paternity. This Judge probably thought, "What the [expletive deleted]? We have a 70-something guy and 50-something woman, and we have a paternity issue?" In any event, he signed the order and sealed the file, and she became Vicky Carol George officially.

We see each other frequently on holidays and at other times. Vicky is now with the Choctaw Indian Tribe working in IT, having recently retired from Legal Shield. During college at East Central in Ada, she had worked putting information into computers for Sears. That got her a start in the IT field. Trained as an accountant, when she started at Prepaid Legal, she was one of only eight employees. When she retired recently from Legal Shield, there were seven hundred employees, and ninety of them reported to her. I told her that this success came from picking the right parents. That is my story, and I am sticking to it.

Number One Son Richard

Our son Richard Peyton George was born in 1970. He

attended St. Agnes grade school and St. Stephens High School in Alexandria VA.

Richard is the Chief Technology Officer and Co-Founder of Empire State Greenhouses LLC, a sixteen million plus carbon negative Food-Energy-Waste project under development in Cobleskill New York that will build a 400,000+ SF carbon negative greenhouse, vertical farm, food processing, and cold storage facility in Cobleskill, NY next to the campus of SUNY Cobleskill. This facility will be powered by a 1.8 MW biogas digester, 10 MW of gasifier syngas fed CHP generators, and 4 MW of solar that use dairy manure, agricultural, food, and forest wastes to produce energy, fertilizers, compost, and biochar. It supports daily truckload food production packed for grocery chain sales as well as aggregation of produce from farms in a 4-hour drive radius. He developed ESG's integrated carbon negative Food-Energy-Waste system and is responsible for its design, engineering, optimization, and research. He also works closely with ESG's finance and development teams to select sites and get project locations through the development steps required to evaluate and select sites, secure economic development incentives, determine site infrastructure requirements, develop site plans, complete designs, and secure all required permits and approvals.

Richard has developed, financed, advised, and/or evaluated over 600 solar photovoltaic energy projects ranging in scale from small commercial systems to megawatt scale utility projects in California, Hawaii, Oregon, New Jersey, Massachusetts, Virginia, Tennessee, Puerto Rico, Louisiana, New York, and Connecticut. He has worked with a broad spectrum of renewable energy technologies: solar thermal; solar concentrators; solar air conditioners;

energy storage; energy efficiency; LED grow lights; building control systems; Nano window coatings; geothermal; fuel cells; biomass; wind; and waste-to-energy technologies. He has been a consultant to multiple solar integration and project development companies, helping them evaluate renewable energy technologies, manage vendors for PV panels and inverters, analyze potential acquisition targets, and evaluate competitors. He also assists clients with data mining installation data, navigating incentive programs, developing investment strategies, and structuring PPA transactions of more than $40 million.

Richard has also worked on multiple regenerative agriculture and food processing projects designing, planning, and implementing commercial scale projects using the Regrarians Platform. Recent projects include developing the technical plans for Empire State Greenhouses, evaluating farm sites for Chobe Advisers, working on a 43,000-acre grazing and meat processing project for Castagno Capital, advising a dairy aggregation and meat processing project for Rumiano Cheese, and designing and implementing the design for a research farm in Tennessee. He also owns and operates a regenerative agriculture farm in Tennessee.

Richard has also worked as a Consulting Manager at KPMG where he provided strategy and technology consulting to a variety of clients, with an additional focus on business development. Prior to joining KPMG, he was COO of Galileo Projects, consultant at DRA Research on best practices and systems to manage the risks of derivatives. At Enron Capital & Trade Resources, he provided valuation, risk, and structuring analysis multi-billion-dollar deals for refinery projects, Canadian oil, and an electric utility acquisition.

Richard holds a doctorate in philosophy from Capella University School of Business and Technology, an MBA from the Haas Graduate School of Business at the University of California at Berkeley, and a BS from the McIntire School of Commerce at the University of Virginia. He is also a Certified Permaculture Designer by the Permaculture Research Institute and has completed the Regrarians regenerative agriculture farm planning program.

Tales, Trips, and Characters

Strike A Match

Two of my Latta High School Classmates, Corkie Hudson and Wayne Tiner, were about 16 years old at the time. They ran out of gas late one night in Corkie's old International Pickup. They eventually obtained some gasoline. In those days one had to prime the carburetor by literally pouring gasoline into it. Corkie was pouring gasoline into the carburetor in the darkness. He told Wayne to strike a match to see where it was going. The pickup became instant history.

Out of Gas

My friend Don Brock—whom I served with at the USDA and who had two hundred acres of asparagus in El Centro, California—tells the story of driving his mother's new Buick as a teenager. He ran out of gas. He called back to the farm to have one of the Mexican hands bring some gasoline. When the worker arrived and started to pour gas into the tank, Don stopped him. He told the worker that this new car only used ethyl (now high-test). The Mexican replied, "Don, when you are out of gas it is all ethyl."

A Plumber's Wisdom

While finishing the basement in my residence in Alexandria, Virginia, in the seventies, a plumber friend and his helper were installing the fixtures in a new bathroom. I was complimenting them on an excellent job. The helper remarked that there were only three things one had to know to be a plumber. I asked what those were, and he replied, "Hot on the left, cold on the right, and [expletive deleted] don't run up hill."

Drywall

We were living at 600 Fort Williams Parkway, Alexandria, Virginia. My son Richard was about five years old, and we were in the process of finishing the same basement in my residence. It was taking an inordinate amount of time putting in partitions and putting up the drywall. I was spackling the cracks in the sheetrock, and Richard would help.

We were both a little weak on our technique, which caused us to leave some very rough places. Some weeks later I became terribly busy at work and did not have the time needed to finish the project. I called a contractor friend and asked if he had some workers whom I might get to finish the drywall work in the basement. He did, and arrangements were made to help finish this job.

I will never forget the evening I arrived home after their first day. The workers had spent most of the day cleaning up my mess so that they could finish the job properly. One was an elderly Black gentleman in his sixties who was clearly a professional in his own right. He addressed me with his hands on his hips and said, "Mr. George, I promise that I will never try to represent myself in court if you will promise me that you will never do drywall again." Fifty years later, after some practice, I sometimes patch drywall as the volunteer handyman for the local senior citizen center.

A Magician

A number of years ago my wife Nancy and I attended a joint meeting in Denver of the Republican Eagles and a Jewish Republican donor group. I was seated with four of the latter attendees, each of whom was a mega-millionaire shopping center owner. One attendee at my table said to another "Moshe, what is that son of yours doing now?" Moshe replied, "My son is a magician. He takes money and makes it disappear."

Sir Geoffrey Archer

In 1975, my office was at 1701 Pennsylvania Avenue NW in Washington, D.C. My friend Paul Lamberth, whom I had worked with in the FBI, was on a retainer from a British author named Sir Geoffrey Archer. Archer had authored several books and was now researching a new book which later became Shall We Tell the President? Archer was a Member of the British Parliament. The three of us went to lunch at Nick and Dottie's, then a restaurant on 17th Street at Pennsylvania Avenue by my office. We spent a fun two-hours during which Archer would toss out hypothetical situations. Then he would ask Paul and me to respond as to how the average FBI agent on the street might react or what they might have said. He gave one hypothetical to which my response was, "Deny the allegation and defy the alligator." He used my response in his book as a quote for one of his principal characters.

Paul Stephen Spielberg

I first heard of Major Paul Spielberg when I was a staff judge advocate (an Army lawyer) with the 352nd Civil Affairs Command. I next heard of the matter some two or three months later when I was in my new job. Colonel Tony Sarbanes, the Chief of Staff, came to me with the Spielberg file and asked me to investigate the matter. We were flying to Charlottesville, Virginia, on one of the 97th U.S Army Reserve Command helicopters with Brigadier General Wayne Jackson and his staff. Our purpose was to visit the 10th Military Law Center Judge Advocate units that were conducting their annual training at the Judge Advocate General's School in Charlottesville. Since I was about to be transferred to the 97th U.S Army Reserve Command, I had been invited to come along.

Sitting beside me was Sam Brick, a Department of Defense bureaucrat. Brick was the acting staff judge advocate at the 97th ARCOM. Brick was reading a file concerning an individual named Spielberg. He was gleeful about what they were going to do to screw this guy, what a big criminal he was, and so on. He showed me the FBI interview reports. I read them, and they were unremarkable. I gave little thought to the matter until after I became the staff judge advocate for that command. At that time, I realized that this was the same case that Sam Brick had spoken of a few months earlier.

I learned that Paul Stephen Spielberg was a Vietnam veteran who had about every ribbon one could have without dying. He had gone on to become a businessman in Chicago. His business, a bar, had gotten into financial trouble and had been taken over by organized crime elements. Spielberg became an undercover FBI informant during this process.

When the matter finally terminated, the FBI considered placing him in the witness protection program. Instead, with the help of the FBI, he chose to go back on active duty with the Army. He was assigned to a post in North Carolina as the active-duty advisor to a problem Army Reserve Special Forces unit. Spielberg, in effect, was running the unit 28 days a month, and the Reserve commander was running it two days a month on the drill weekend.

Judging from the initial reports, Spielberg was doing a bang-up job cleaning up a problem unit. This unit had been out of control for some time. The reserve unit members would go to the arms room and get military weapons to go deer hunting and do other things which were forbidden by Army regulations. Spielberg's efficiency reports started going from exceptionally good to extremely poor. A personality clash had developed with the reserve commander, who was jealous of Spielberg's activities.

Spielberg allegedly talked to some members of the unit trying to recruit them to go on a mission back to Chicago to kidnap an organized crime figure, make him tell all, and then turn the information over to the federal government for a reward. According to Spielberg, he was just thinking aloud. The commander of the unit used this information to call in the FBI for a big investigation and used this as an excuse to get rid of Spielberg. The FBI investigation developed that nothing had really transpired, and the U.S. Attorney refused to prosecute.

At that point, the Reserve commander tried hard to

try to get action taken by higher headquarters. Spielberg was placed on administrative leave and was left in this small town in North Carolina with nothing to do. Spielberg, being the enterprising person that he was, had opened a restaurant known as Joanne's Chili Bordello that received considerable notoriety. The problem continued to fester for months because no one at the headquarters had balls enough to place Spielberg in another assignment. Adding to the problem, he had also been previously crosswise with the unionized civilian reserve technician bureaucrats.

Spielberg had been doing nothing for the Army for about six months when a news story broke about an active-duty Army major running a restaurant. The Army finally ordered Spielberg to Fort Meade, Maryland. There he would spend five days a week sitting at a desk with nothing to do. The suspicion of being involved in organized crime had accompanied Spielberg to Fort Meade. He would drive back home to North Carolina on weekends.

One day, some technician looked in the window of Spielberg's office and saw Spielberg with a pistol. It turned out to be a personally owned weapon that he was taking back to his home in North Carolina. But this person ran to headquarters claiming that Spielberg was going to commit suicide. The MPs were called, and Spielberg was carted off to Walter Reed Army Medical Center for examination. It was at this point that Colonel Sarbanes asked me to investigate the matter. It was then that I learned about organized crime taking over his bar in Chicago and his service as an FBI informant.

I interviewed the person who claimed that Spielberg was trying to commit suicide, and I asked him all the right questions. Did Spielberg have the gun? What do you mean he is trying to kill himself? Did Spielberg have the gun to his head? Was the gun loaded? Did he have the gun in his mouth? What makes you think that he was going to kill himself? All the guy would say was, "Oh, he was just going to kill himself, he was just going to kill himself." That allegation washed out fast.

I spoke to the psychiatrists at Walter Reed who were examining him. They said that there was nothing wrong with this guy mentally, but he was angry by what everybody was trying to do to him. They intended to release him. I spoke to the FBI agents in Chicago who had used Spielberg as an informant. One of the agents commented that Spielberg was the "bravest, most patriotic S.O.B. he had ever met." He said he would rather have one Spielberg than ten of anyone else as informants. I rapidly concluded that Spielberg was being shafted. Further complicating this matter, the 11th Special Forces commander, another DoD bureaucrat named James Willoughby, was a close neighbor of General Wayne Jackson, the commander of the 97th Army Reserve Command. Willoughby was a colossal petty DoD bureaucratic jerk. He continued lobbying Jackson to take drastic action against Spielberg. He even sued me for supporting Spielberg, a case that was promptly dismissed.

I wrote up a summary of what my investigations had revealed and recommended that Spielberg be given another reserve assignment in another location. They failed to follow my advice and finally ordered Spielberg back to his unit at the reserve center in North Carolina. Predictably, with all the tension and anxiety, Spielberg became embroiled in an argument with one of the civilian technicians over the turning off the air conditioning system.

Spielberg was again ordered to leave the center. An AR 15-6 investigation was eventually conducted. This is a fact-finding administrative inquiry.

Privately, Colonel Paul Kite, senior Active Army advisor at the ARCOM, had been supportive of Spielberg. He too saw the case as a personality clash that had just gotten blown out of proportion. Spielberg later told me that Jack McNiff, who was one of the technicians and an Army veteran at the headquarters, was very cordial and supportive, while most of the other people treated him like the plague. I gave great deference to his situation.

Colonel Kite called me one Sunday for a meeting about Spielberg at the ARCOM Headquarters at Fort Meade. When I arrived, it turned out to be a roast of Colonel Peyton George, staff judge advocate. The room was filled with the head civilian technicians and his entourage of civilian bureaucrats, and Colonel Kite, the senior Army advisor. All of them were attacking me because I had advised the commander not to take any action against Spielberg. I became so disgusted with the whole bunch that I went home and wrote out a letter addressed to Colonel Paul Kite. He retired upon receipt, and we saved Major Spielberg. While at times a little rough around the edges, to me, Spielberg was the kind of officer we should tolerate in peace time because we certainly want him available when we go to war.

G. Gordon Liddy

On February 9, 1994, Larry Whitt, Vice President of Pizza Hut, Pam Sederholm, with the Advocates for Flexible Employment trade association, and I were having dinner at the Blue Point Restaurant in Old Town Alexandria.

Once seated at our table, I recognized a gentleman who came in with his wife and sat down as G. Gordon Liddy, a former FBI agent of Watergate Fame who had gone to jail. He now had his own syndicated talk show. I put a note on one of my cards that read, "From some of your fans, Larry Whitt, VP Pizza Hut, Pam Sederholm, and Peyton George, ex-FBI agent." I gave it to the waitress and told her to go tell him that we would like to buy him and his wife a drink.

A brief time later, the waitress returned with my card. Liddy had written on the back, "Thank you, sir! Unfortunately, I am no longer allowed by the medics to drink (blood pressure). Warm wishes, G. Gordon Liddy (It is grapefruit juice.)"

James McCord

Jim McCord was the head of security for the Committee to Re-elect the President (CREEP), which ran the second Nixon campaign in 1972. In the spring of 1972, my wife received a call at home from an individual who identified himself as Jim McCord. He wanted to talk to me about a job. He had obtained my résumé from the Society of Former FBI Agents at the time. After the Kennedy assassination, I had been loaned from time to time as an FBI agent to the Secret Service until they could beef up their staff. I assume they had this in their dossier.

I was whisked back and forth in John Mitchell's limousine from the Department of Agriculture to 1701 Pennsylvania Avenue, the headquarters of the Committee to Re-elect the President, for my various meetings with Jim McCord. McCord told me that I had been selected to be the bodyguard for Martha Mitchell, the wife of the former Attorney General John Mitchell. Mitchell was heading up the committee, and his wife liked the agents that were around them when he was attorney general. Her bodyguard had to be a former FBI agent within a certain age bracket. Apparently, they had done a CIA profile on me. I was from Oklahoma, Mrs. Mitchell was from Arkansas, and the CIA thought we could probably get along.

My first reaction was that I wanted no part of this because I had done that type of work eight years earlier on the LBJ protection detail and certainly did not want to go back to it. I finally told McCord, who was very insistent, that if they wanted to make me an associate in the law firm of Mitchell, Mudge, Rose and Alexander, I would be the best darn wife sitter, wife muzzler, or whatever they wanted for the remaining several months of the campaign. That was the only way I could justify this professionally. His response was, "Sounds fine to me. You gotta meet Fred LaRue."

My wife came with me the following Saturday to LaRue's office at the Committee to Re-elect the President. LaRue was Mitchell's right-hand man. It turns out he had gone to the University of Oklahoma (OU), as had my wife, and they chitchatted about OU activities. Then LaRue turned to me and remarked that McCord had told him what I wanted. He wanted me to run through it again, so I gave him my story. His response: "Sounds fine to me. I'll take it up with Mr. Mitchell." A few days later, McCord called to say that Mitchell had rejected the idea because they already had too many people working on the campaign from the law firm. They had to show salaries as contributions. He begged me to consider that I would not have to work very much, except when she was traveling, and that he could put me on the rolls of his own private investigative firm. I would certainly make as much money as I was making as a GS15 at USDA.

I told him that I would not consider it under any other circumstances, at which point he remarked that I knew what they wanted and asked, "Who would you recommend?" I told him to call Steve King, or Bob McKenna, two contemporaries from the Washington Field Office of the FBI. Both were then working on subcommittees on Capitol Hill. He eventually hired Steve King, who would become the one accused of holding Mrs. Mitchell while she was given a shot after she went berserk upon learning of the Watergate break-in.

Several weeks later in early June, I happened to be in town after constant travel on the presidential campaign. I was taking my wife and two-year-old son to the Watergate Concert, which was then down at Memorial Bridge. Military bands used to play along the waterfront. That is where Watergate got its name. About 7PM on a Friday evening, I stopped into Howard Johnson's hotel across the street from the Watergate to get my son an ice cream cone.

Upon entering Howard Johnson's and walking up to the counter, I spotted my new best friend, Jim McCord, sitting across a couple rows of counters. He promptly hopped up and came around and engaged me in a conversation. In hindsight, I realized Barker and all the others were with him there for a last dinner before the break in. He told me what a fantastic job Steve King was doing and that he was out at San Clemente that evening with Mrs. Mitchell. He wanted to know if I needed a place to stay at the Republican Convention in Florida. I told him I did not, that I did not plan to go, whereupon he left the restaurant.

I thought it was unusual that he did not pay a check. When I got outside with my son and his ice cream cone, I asked my wife if she had seen McCord cross the street. I assumed that he was there because the Mitchells lived in the Watergate. She indicated that no one had come out the door.

The press report did not come out until Sunday morning. It happened to be an Army Reserve weekend, and I was sitting in the back of a deuce-and-a-half Army truck at the firing range at Fort Meade. I was reading the Washington Post, and I had this sick feeling as I started reading about the break-in. That got me interviewed by the FBI and written up in a couple of Watergate books: The Secret Agenda by Jim Hougan and The Silent Coup: The Removal of a President by Len Colodny. It seems that actor Burt Lancaster, me, and the Watergate burglars all crossed paths within seconds of one another in the lobby of that Howard Johnson's.

Jim Traficant

While working as a lawyer and lobbyist for the Wendy's restaurant chain in Washington, D.C., one of my responsibilities was to stay connected with the Ohio Congressional delegation since they could usually be relied on if we had a problem because Wendy's is head-quartered in that state. Usually, I worked with the law department or the general counsel, but occasionally the government relations role would get assigned to other company representatives.

For a brief period, Debbie Mitchell, a Vice President for Finance, I believe, was assigned to government relations. She came to Washington, and I took her around to meet members of the Ohio Delegation. One of these was Congressman Jim Traficant. He was a very colorful individual and later went to prison for taking kickbacks or bribes. He was always helpful to us, and he would always tell us whether he could support us or not, since he came from a big union area.

I took Debbie Mitchell in to introduce her to the Congressman. He was a great big bear of a man. Debbie was not much more than five feet tall and was wearing her prim and proper dress-for-success outfit. I said, "Congressman, I would like you to meet the new Vice President of Wendy's, who handles government relations," whereupon he said, "Come here, you little hamburger, you," and gave her a great big bear hug. I wish I had a photograph of her face at the time. It was just utter shock and disbelief.

Waterloo, Iowa

When I was about 14 years old, I won the first prize at the county fair with my Holstein milk cow named Nancy. This got me an all-expenses-paid trip to the National Dairy Congress in Waterloo, Iowa. Three other boys and I went with the County Agent Cy Hailey, who drove five of us in a two-door coupe to Iowa. The high point of the trip for me was touring a John Deere factory plant.

Caracas, Venezuela, and Margarita Island

In 1971, my wife Nancy and I left our son Richard with neighbors Jim and Beth Nelson and went to visit my friends Robert and Sylvia Cavanaugh. Bob and I worked together in the FBI in D.C. They were living in Caracas, Venezuela. Bob was with the police training part of the Agency for International Development (AID). Judging from all the people I met at his cocktail parties, I presumed he was probably with the Central Intelligence Agency at the time.

We spent two weeks there. Bob and I rode his Italian Moto Guzzi motorcycle all over Caracas. We visited collectable art-glass plants and the racetrack where the famous racehorse Canonero II had run. I especially remember seeing signs in the stores in Caracas that read "Sale, New York Prices."

Nancy and I took a side flight to Margarita Island on the Venezuelan airline. This was the era of many hijackings to Cuba. Airline security back then in Venezuela consisted of the pilot holding a machine gun on the passengers while the co-pilot frisked them. They did not have a lot of hijacking problems at that airline.

Amsterdam

In the mid-seventies, my friend, Joe Hillings, then a Vice President of National Airlines, got me on a National Airlines Inaugural flight from New York JFK to Amsterdam. The other guests were mayors and other officials up and down the East Coast. We were wined and dined for a week in Amsterdam. We were exposed to symphonies, art galleries with art by the old Dutch masters, and tours. A fabulous trip and experience.

Paris, Venice, and the Orient Express

In the 1980s, I took my wife, our son, my mother-in-law, and my parents to Paris. From there, we boarded the Orient Express train from Paris to Venice. It was a great trip. My wife and I got dressed up, me in a tuxedo and she in dinner attire, each evening for dinner. We stayed at the outstanding Daniela Hotel in Venice and flew back to the U.S. from Rome.

Buenos Aires, Argentina and Iguazu Falls, Brazil

In 1988, our son graduated from St. Stephens High School in Alexandria, Virginia, and went off to the University of Virginia. My wife and I had frequent flier miles amassed over the years and wanted to use them. We looked on the map and asked ourselves, "Where is the farthest we can go and go First Class?" We ended up flying to Buenos Aires, Argentina, and to Santiago, Chile, for a couple of weeks—a trip of a lifetime.

Prices at the time were cheap in both Argentina and Chile. A great dinner for two could be enjoyed for $25 to $30. The best bottle of wine on the menu cost about eight dollars. We decided to take an internal trip on the Argentine Domestic Airline, Avianca, to Iguazu Falls on the Amazon River, where Argentina, Paraguay and Brazil join. We spent the night at a resort on the Argentine side. The next day, we hired a guide who took us, probably illegally, through a part of Paraguay and across the Amazon to the Brazilian side.

We were climbing down the stairs to view the falls when a Japanese tourist bumped into my wife, causing her to trip and turn her ankle. I took her back up to the outdoor café at the resort on the Brazilian side and got a bag of ice for her ankle. Since I was already there, I decided to go ahead alone and take the helicopter ride over the falls.

It was me and several Japanese tourists. It was a little unnerving that they kept a five-gallon gas can near the helicopter. Each trip, they would put another five gallons of gas in the helicopter. That way they could carry an extra passenger with almost no excess fuel on board. Flying over the falls was a wonderful experience. It is much larger than our own Niagara Falls and breathtaking. The helicopter ride cost $20.

After my helicopter ride, I returned to the resort and retrieved my wife. We started our trek back to the Argentine side, stopping at several shops along the way. Our flight to Buenos Aires arrived late in the afternoon. At that time, my wife's foot had swelled even more. We did not know if it was broken or not. She wanted an X-ray. We went to our hotel, the Elevage, and the doorman put us in another taxi to get an X-ray. We were first driven to a mental hospital. We found they did not do X-rays there. We got back in the cab, and the driver took us to a maternity hospital. We found out they did not do X-rays there either. Finally, we learned that one went to a special location that just did X-rays.

We found it on the ground floor of a high-rise office building. My wife threw a complete fit, insisting that she see a doctor. The X-ray technicians finally went upstairs in this high rise building and returned with a doctor. The doctor held her ankle while it was being X-rayed. I thought this was a little strange.

My wife thought that if she spoke louder in English, the Spanish speakers would understand her. She kept talking in "pidgin English" to this doctor, asking if her foot was broken. He was looking at her as if she were a nut case. Finally, in frustration, she jerks a wooden pencil out of the doctor's shirt pocket, breaks it, and points at her foot and says, "Foot broken?" The doctor in perfect English said, "No, Mrs. George, your foot is not broken. You have a severe sprain. You've done all the right things by putting ice on it." We got a big laugh out of that one. I paid him $20 and learned that he had gone to Harvard Medical School.

He gave us a recommendation for a great Italian restaurant called La Cosa Nostra. As a former FBI Agent, I had to go there. We got back into another cab in the pouring rain and went to the restaurant he had recommended for dinner. Part of our problem with information, in addition to us not speaking Spanish, was that this was a holiday. The American Embassy and other places where we could have gotten better directions were not available.

Argentina was being settled by European immigrants at the same time the United States was being settled. Buenos Aires has huge Italian sections, English sections, and German sections. I took the hydrofoil over to Colonia, Uruguay, by myself the next day. It was close by, and my wife's foot kept her from traveling for a day or two.

In Buenos Aires, the subways had been built by the Germans many years earlier. They were rickety and sometimes ran with the doors off. In Santiago, Chile, their subways, and their downtown were very modern contrasted with Buenos Aires. In Argentina it seemed that most of the cars were old Ford Falcons. In Santiago, Chile, cars were mostly new Mercedes and Jaguars.

Santiago, Chile

A few years earlier, the Chilean military had bombed the

presidential palace to get rid of Allende, the communist president. I was tremendously impressed that their military could destroy their capitol building from the air without damaging any of the high-rise buildings on either side. Our folks would have leveled the whole downtown.

Santiago had great shopping and great restaurants. The emphasis was on seafood as opposed to beef in Argentina. I had been advised by one of my friends, Mike Letellier, a former FBI legal attaché in Chile, that we should visit Vina del Mar on the coast. We hired a driver and a van one Sunday morning to take us on the two-hour ride to Valparaiso and adjacent Vina del Mar. Valparaiso was the port, and Vina del Mar was the resort and the beach venue. It was a beautiful drive through the wine country in Chile.

Once at Vina del Mar, we drove up and down along the beach. We saw the equivalent of Beach Week for affluent Chilean college kids and watched frolicking sea lions in the Pacific Ocean. It was wall-to-wall people as one would see in Ocean City, Maryland, in the summer. We visited a casino, and later we decided to stay in Vina Del Mar for dinner. We chose a great seafood restaurant right on the Pacific Ocean and watched a spectacular sunset.

We were usually at dinner by 7PM. Most of the locals did not go to dinner until 9PM. We usually had the restaurant, at least for the early part of the evening, to ourselves. We received lots of attention from the wait staff and the owner when they learned that we were from the Washington, D.C. area. Soon we were visiting with folks at tables on either side as the restaurant began to fill up.

We had a fabulous $35 seafood dinner and a bottle of the Concha Y Toro 83. Since we still had a two-hour drive back through the wine country to our hotel in Santiago, we wanted a bottle of wine to take with us. We had a tough time translating "take out" into Spanish. With the help of the tables around us, our waiter finally determined what we wanted.

Soon our tuxedoed waiter came out of the kitchen with a silver tray, two glasses and a bottle of wine. When I reached for the bottle, he insisted "No" and said he was going with us to our vehicle. We left the restaurant, followed by our tuxedoed waiter with his tray with the bottle of wine and two glasses on it. We had a couple of blocks to go through wall-to-wall people along the beach to our van. Our van driver, who had been waiting, was completely puzzled by all this. He had been available that Sunday to drive us as he wanted to practice his English. He had plans to visit his cousin in New York City.

Once we were seated in the van, the waiter opened the bottle of wine and poured us each a glass. He then set the wine bottle in the van. I tried to tip him another five dollars, but he insisted that was too much. He thought that we had already tipped in the restaurant. Before leaving the restaurant, the owner had insisted on giving us menus to take with us. He asked that we urge our friends in Washington, D.C. to visit his restaurant.

Italy and the Bergere Family Reunions

For this trip Barbara and I had originally flown into Frankfurt, Germany, where we visited Barbara's daughter and her husband who was assigned to Ramstein Air Force Base. From there we went to Vienna by train to visit another cousin, Susan Cohen, with the International Atomic Energy Commission. She is Australian by birth. She toured us around Vienna, and we saw the Lipizzaner Performance. From there we boarded another train on to Trieste for the family reunion.

We were hosted by local cousins. One cousin was a city council woman. Another Italian cousin was with Fox News in Rome. Barbara's cousin in Zagreb, Croatia, was a world-renowned brain stem-cell researcher, who was trained at Johns Hopkins and taught at the University of California. He was one of the sharpest individuals I have ever met. He lived in a house that Tito had lived in. He hosted us there for lunch and afterwards gave us a walking tour of downtown Zagreb. He would come over to Trieste to events there.

We stayed one night in a castle just outside the City of Zagreb, but in Slovenia. It is now a five-star golf resort. It had been owned by some of the family before World War II. Most of the Bergers (the name used in Europe) decided that being Jewish was not a good business plan, and they sold the castle to the Catholic Church and became Catholics. We had breakfast at the castle with Peter Croker, a top Australian golf pro, and the top Slovenia woman golfer. She was about seven feet tall. We had been at an adjacent table but then joined them. I still get emails from him on occasion. He was there to teach a golf lesson to other golf pros. Barbara and I stopped off in Florence and Rome on the way back to the United States.

In 2006 the European cousins all came to Santa Fe for another reunion. They had been to Santa Fe before Barbara, and I got together. Their family had known that one brother came to America, Barbara's grandfather, Alfred Bergere. The family genealogist eventually located the American cousins. In 2008 the European cousins put on another Berger/Bergere family reunion. This time it started in Liverpool. Barbara and I flew first to Paris since she had never been there. We flew first class on points and stayed in the Hilton Hotel on points wherever we could to hedge against the Euro. The first day in Paris we walked around the Champs-Élysées. The next day we visited the Louvre Museum and took a boat ride on the river Seine.

My friend Stuart Sturm, whom I had recruited for the Former FBI Agents Association when I was chairman of the Recruitment Committee, had been the FBI legal attaché (Legat) in Ottawa. He was then Microsoft's man in Europe and conducted their European investigations. His offices were in Paris, and he had told me to call if I ever went there. I called. He suggested we come out to Microsoft's office on the 37th floor overlooking Paris. He showed us around there, introduced us to the staff, then put us in a car, took us to Versailles and dinner in the countryside. Afterwards, he took us all over Paris at night, dropping us off at our hotel at 1AM. We saw more of Paris in that one day than most people see in weeks.

The following day, we toured the Montmartre area of Paris and then took the Chunnel. This is the train from Paris to London that goes under the English Channel. By coincidence, this was two days before the train caught fire, burning many trucks, and closing the tunnel briefly. We were met by her cousin Michael Berger, the family genealogist, and his wife Maureen. He took us to Windsor Castle and toured us around some. We had lunch at a pub in the countryside, and they then turned us over to cousins Fabio and Lolly Berger. Fabio and Lolly live in both Trieste and in London. Lolly took us into downtown London on the subway for two days for sightseeing. We had lunch with their son, who is a hedge fund manager in London. The third day, we rode with them to Liverpool, where the family reunion officially began.

The hotel we stayed in was adequate but old. It was in its heyday when the Titanic sank. The first afternoon Barbara and I walked out of the hotel across the street to a pub. There we found a band playing "Okie from Muskogee." After a couple of days of sightseeing and touring cemeteries and the schools that her grandfather had attended, we flew to Valencia, Spain, where the Luna family originated. They were allegedly descendants of a pope and had a 65,000-acre Spanish land grant in Los Lunes when Spain owned New Mexico. They ran a huge sheep ranch. They allegedly did sheep drives to the gold miners in California in the 1840s when the cattle drives from Texas to Kansas City seemed to make the movies.

We toured Valencia and went up to Pensacola, where Papa Luna's Castle was located. He was known as Pope Benedict XIII and was in office around 1394 to 1423. At that time Scotland, France and Spain supported him for pope, but the Italians and some other countries supported another pope. He lost out and became the anti-pope. In most of the cathedrals there are still plaques attributed to him.

The rest of the group were going directly to Trieste. Since we had been there four years earlier, we wanted to spend some time in Barcelona. We took most of the tours there and then flew to Naples. We really had no plan on how to get from the Naples airport to Sorrento where I had hotel reservations at the Hilton. When we walked out the door of the airport, there was a bus boarding for Sorrento. It cost about ten dollars, and we were there in an hour.

We only had a brief time in Sorrento to see the Amalfi Coast. The tours began at 8AM in the morning and dropped one off at 6PM. This did not fit our tight schedule, so I had the concierge get us a rental car. The next morning the agency dropped off this tiny little Renault stick-shift car in front of the hotel and left the keys at the front desk. We started down the Amalfi Coast. After about an hour we pulled into a place to take photographs. Afterwards I could not get the car into reverse, so I just put it in neutral, pushed it back out on the street, and we took off.

I have a commercial driver's license and have driven everything on the road, but it had been a long time since I had driven a stick-shift Renault. The next hour or so it was like driving a motorhome; one tries not to get into places one must back out of.

The Amalfi Drive runs down the coast of Italy below Naples. It is a two-lane road, but it is the equivalent of one lane American. Periodically cars are parked on each side of the road, and one must get into a single file. We came around a curve into where we were in a single file just as a huge tour bus came in at the other end. Suddenly, we are sitting headlight to headlight with this big bus. The driver is waving, "Back up, back up," and I am pointing at my gearshift saying, "Reverse broken." The standoff lasted a minute or two. Finally, the driver got out of the bus, jerked my car door open and probably said the only words of English he knew: "Get out." He gets in the car with Barbara, slams it in reverse, goes flying back about one hundred feet, to where he can get his bus through. I asked Barbara, "What happened?"

Barbara said, "Don't ask." There was a ring on the gearshift that we were pushing up instead of pulling down. We got a laugh out of it. I am sure all the people on the bus were complaining about these American geezers over here, clogging our highways. The rest of the day we could park in spots where we had to back out.

The next morning, we took the local train into Naples and then took the fast train to Florence. There we spent the night and did some heavy-duty shopping. The next day we took the train to Trieste and met up with the rest of the group. That evening we had a huge reception at Fabio's flat from the 1700s in downtown Trieste and had a big family dinner at a local restaurant. Next morning, our entire group flew to Prague, the Czech Republic, where the family genealogist had found some more cousins. We had a great tour of Prague and saw some of the outlying areas before flying back to the United States.

The Real Estate Guy I Met in Albuquerque

In May 2016, I went to Mayo Clinic in Phoenix for my annual physical exam. My companion at the time, Susanne Fuqua, and I were returning home to Santa Fe. Suzanne was driving in her vehicle. About twenty miles east of Flagstaff, I received a call from Kevin Daniels, whom I did not know at the time. He reported that presidential candidate Donald Trump was going to do a rally in Albuquerque. He was putting together a private reception, and the cost was $10,000 per person. I told him to stop right there as this was out of my league. I told him that this was a poor state, and he was not going to raise that kind of money. To my surprise, he volunteered that he had two people who were each giving $5,000 but were not attending. We then ended the conversation.

We traveled about another one hundred miles east on Interstate 40 while I thought about his call. I then sent him a text message that read, "I am an old political advance man. I know what you are trying to do on short notice. If this would help you, Suzanne and I would each commit to $1,000 each, and you can pair us with the two guys you mentioned that are giving $5,000 each but are not coming." We had driven about another hundred miles when I received another phone call from Daniels. He said, "You're in."

Suzanne and I attended the private reception with Donald Trump in a room off the convention hall in Albuquerque. There were twenty-five attendees. Most were hedge fund guys from Dallas who had flown in on their private jets. Everyone had a table tent with their name on it, and the tables formed a large square. Trump went around to everyone, greeting each person by name. For example, "Peyton, who do you suggest for Vice President?" "Suzanne, who do you suggest?" He was very personable and gave a nice talk. He then posed for photos with any of the Albuquerque Police Officers who wanted one. Several were in riot gear. Being a former police officer, I thought this was really a class act. He then took individual photos with all the contributors.

After Trump made a few more remarks we could hear the crowd in the convention hall next door getting revved up. Trump then stood up and said, "Well, I gotta go put on a show" and promptly went out and attacked the governor for being a "no show." We stayed in the back of the convention hall for a while and listened to his talk. We could have sat up behind him, but we did not want to get caught in traffic. There were numerous demonstrators and troublemakers outside.

We left the Convention Center and walked through the middle of all the protestors. Once we got past them, there were a couple of young Mexican guys with a big poster that read, "Not all Mexicans are Criminals. Hug a Mexican!" I told Suzanne to go over and hug that kid with the poster. She did, and I took a photo. Then he came over and hugged me. They were just having a fun time and were not part of the batch of demonstrators.

At the reception, I met some people from the Republican National Committee, whom I had had contact with before. I parlayed that into going to the Republican Convention in Cleveland, Ohio, with Suzanne. My friend Steve King ran the convention and provided access to everything. Steve and I were FBI agents together in the 1960s in the FBI Washington, D.C. Field Office. As I mentioned before, he took the job as Martha Mitchell's bodyguard when I turned it down during the 1972 Presidential campaign. Steve went on to be a business guy in Wisconsin and a Republican national committeeman. He later became the U.S. Ambassador to the Czech Republic during the Trump Administration.

In Cleveland, at the Republican Convention, we stayed at the same hotel as the Trump kids. When we checked in, Senator Jeff Sessions checked in at the same time. We chatted with him briefly. Each morning at breakfast we would join the Trump kids. They were sharp people. Most other attendees did not seem to get up that early. We were in the premier viewing spot at the convention and located with all the dignitaries. Suzanne had photos taken with many of them.

Subsequently, Suzanne and I attended all the inaugural events in D.C. First, we attended the Texas Black-Tie and Boots Ball. It is much more fun than the regular inaugural ball. We took my son and daughter-in-law to that one. The following night we took my son and my 14-year-old granddaughter to the regular inaugural ball. This was the best of all the inaugurals I have been fortunate enough to attend, including Nixon, Reagan, and the Bushes. After the 2020 pandemic I doubt there will ever be another inaugural with large crowds and world-class entertainment.

Lawyer Reciprocity

In years past, based upon passing the Virginia Bar Exam, I was admitted to practice in the District of Columbia and Oklahoma thanks to the concept of reciprocity, which most states have. When I moved to New Mexico to retire, with some help from my friends, I became very much involved in obtaining lawyer reciprocity for New Mexico, which it did not have.

Shortly after arriving, I became interested in the New Mexico's lack of lawyer reciprocity issue when an inmate was lost in the Santa Fe County Jail for three years. The public defender had quit, and the prosecutor had lost track. This chap was just stuck in the county jail, without trial, and on some serious charges. It became a bit of a scandal when this surfaced in the press. The judge was upset. The issue was a shortage of public defenders. I contacted the judge and offered to help, as I had some discretionary time. The judge referred me to the then head public defender for New Mexico. I met with this chap, or twit, and explained that I wanted to help, I did not want or need any money, and though I did not consider myself a big defense lawyer, I had handled several such matters in the past. I told him I would be happy to help with lesser cases, so the full-time staff could concentrate on more serious ones. I explained that I was a former Oklahoma City Police Officer, a Former FBI Agent, a former partner in two different 200-lawyer law firms, was a retired Army JAG colonel with 34 years active duty and reserve time, and that I was an active member of the Virginia, District of Columbia, and Oklahoma Bars. This chap looked at me and snidely remarked that I was not a member of the New Mexico Bar. He said they might use me sometime as a paralegal on some financial matters.

He and his staff were obviously much more interested in preserving their New Mexico bar protectionist cabal than providing much needed competent defense to indigent defendants. I was appalled by such a response and walked out of his office. I started checking into how bad things really were in New Mexico in this area. Their protectionism also adversely affected New Mexico Bar members who wanted or needed to relocate to other jurisdictions. Mexican lawyers (with only an undergraduate degree) under NAFTA could practice in New Mexico with reciprocity but not lawyers from other American states without taking another redundant, expensive bar exam.

I met with Tim Burr and obtained material he had used to obtain reciprocity in Arizona a year or two earlier. At the time, Burr was a law professor at Arizona State University. I had numerous meetings with New Mexico Bar personnel. I wrote letters to the New Mexico Supreme Court and the Bar committees. My letters were mostly ignored, except for occasional responses from Justice Daniels of the New Mexico Supreme Court.

Pat Rogers, a lawyer in Albuquerque, weighed in, and we filed a suit with the New Mexico Supreme Court signed by twenty-six members of the New Mexico Bar. Our suit advocated the simple and easy to manage American Bar Association (ABA) reciprocity rule. I filed the suit in the New Mexico Supreme Court clerk's office, paid the filing fee, and had it date stamped as filed.

The next day, the clerk's office called and told me to come and get it. They had unfiled it and with no explanation. Welcome to the way courts work in New Mexico. One business guy commented at the time that New Mexico was a third-world country masquerading as a state. One can only compare it with the State of Arizona to see the difference. Both became states at the same time. One is booming; the other is at the bottom in most ratings.

I spoke with Paul Gessing of the Rio Grande Foundation, and his organization weighed in with some articles. Eventually, the Examiners who had consistently opposed reciprocity came in with their convoluted proposal after being smoked out. We are stuck with that for now. It has outrageous filing fees and several other onerous restrictions. For example, one must have taken the Multi-State Professional Responsibility Exam (MPRE) within five years. I had taken it earlier when I thought I might try to get admitted in Arizona. I went to the University of New Mexico law school for the test as it was more convenient. At the time, 77-year-old me was in the room with all these 20-something-kids. I happily studied well for the test by completing an internet course on the subject.

When those who monitored the test called time, I was still going back and re-checking answers. Based on a scaled score, I scored 111. Most states require a score of 75 to 85. In simple terms, I aced it. When I later applied for reciprocity in New Mexico, my score was six months too old for their rules, another of several absurd and costly requirements. I doubt that people automatically and abruptly forget everything at the end of five years. Reciprocity is about not taking redundant exams that have been taken before.

I weighed in on this hang-up with the New Mexico Supreme Court. I explained that I was on the Santa Fe County Ethics Board, and that I got an outstanding score on their Multi-state Professional Responsibility Exam, essentially an ethics test. The court surprisingly gave me an official court order, despite the Bar Examiners rule, accepting my overdue MPRE score. New Mexico's brand of reciprocity still includes some costly hurdles designed to exclude competent, experienced applicants but I was in the first group admitted through reciprocity.

During the ordeal, I had to deal with the National Conference of Bar Examiners (NCBE), leaving me with the perception that it was a dysfunctional organization. They do support a system that, in some states that refuse to grant reciprocity, is somewhat of a shakedown of some who do not have much money. Universal reciprocity would perhaps curtail their cabal that tries to drag out the admission process.

I was trying to meet a deadline for the first group of admittees under the new reciprocity rules. At the last minute, NCBE claimed they needed a notarized statement from the Virginia State Police and one from the New Mexico State Police, as I had lived in both jurisdictions. The New Mexico Police one came through promptly. I kept checking on the one from Virginia. I would call the Virginia State Police, and they would say they had never received anything from the bar examiners. The NCBE would claim they sent the request to Virginia State Police, a lie. Finally, I called retired Captain Dennis Robertson whom I had helped get his job back in 1962 and told him my problem. He said his daughter worked there and he would get on that first thing the next day. The next morning, I received a call from the head of personnel for the Virginia State Police. She said she still had received nothing from the Bar examiners. As far as I know they still have not. She asked me to send her whatever form I had sent NCBE, which I faxed to her. She called right back and told me it would be taken care of that day. Never burn bridges. It sometimes pays to have friends in the right places when dealing with such bureaucracies.

I now have an advocacy group, Lawyers United. We take on this reciprocity issue nationwide. My colleagues there were quite impressed with my results in New Mexico. We advocate for reciprocity in federal and state courts. I also sometimes front for lawyer spouses of military members through The Military Spouse JD Network. This group is for those who are unlucky enough to have their spouse transferred to some protectionist jurisdiction with burdensome admission requirements. One person can make a difference—especially if one is not concerned who one offends in doing so.

The United States District Court of New Mexico (USDC-NM) required one to take the New Mexico Bar to practice in their federal court. I was admitted to the Western District of Oklahoma's U.S. District Court, and they accepted New Mexico federal bar members. I started a letter writing campaign to Judge Martha Vasquez, a Santa Fe Federal Judge who was sympathetic. I would see her at cocktail parties and complain about this issue. Her then husband, Joe Maestas, was my city counselor. I would write to the Chief Judge in Albuquerque, but never receive any response.

One day, I got a letter back from Judge Vasquez telling me she knew how frustrated I was and that she had provided all my material to the other judges. This gave me an opening to send another letter to Vasquez. I had copied all the other Federal Judges in New Mexico. I also faxed a copy to then Chief Judge Armijo's Chambers in Albuquerque at 3PM on a Monday afternoon. The letter had set out all the many times that I had tried to contact her and had sent Federal Express envelopes with our materials suing other courts and judges over this issue.

Barbara, my life partner at the time, and I landed in Baltimore the next morning for a retired Army JAG convention. When I turned on my cell phone, I had a frantic message from the Chief Federal Judge's secretary. When I returned the call, she said the Judge wanted to meet with me. I told her I was out of town for two weeks. She put Chief Judge Armijo on the phone. I am a nobody, but here I was, walking around the BWI airport, talking to the Chief Federal Judge in New Mexico. I asked Judge Armijo if she had been reading all that stuff I had been sending for months. She said she had and wanted to meet with me. I told her I was out of town for two weeks. She told me to call as soon as I returned.

Two weeks later, I had a very charming meeting with her and her court clerk in her conference room. As I got up to leave, I mentioned that I had had dinner with Fletcher Catron, Barbara's cousin, the night before. I knew that she knew him. She lit up like a Christmas tree and told me to wait there. She went into her office next to the conference room and obviously took a picture off the wall. She brought it back to the conference room. It was a photo of her father, who was Chief Justice of the New Mexico Supreme Court back in about the 1920s or 1930s. Anyone who was anybody in New Mexico at the time was in that photo. She pointed out all the people to me by name. She must have thought I was a New Mexico historian.

I had told her in our meeting that if we had to sue, she would be the defendant and be out of the case. Then another federal judge would have to come in and clean up the admission rules. To her credit she set out to fix the matter. Every few weeks she would give me a personal call to provide an update on where they were with the rule changes. Eventually it got finalized, and I was admitted to the federal Bar in New Mexico before being admitted to the NM state Bar. It again shows that one person can make a difference. Only one-third of the Federal Trial Courts (USDCs) have reciprocity, while two-thirds want to protect their local lawyers from competition. This can often deny the client access to the best and brightest or make it very costly. A member of any state bar can walk into the U.S. Supreme Court or the Circuit Courts of Appeal. Go figure.

Santa Fe County Ethics Board

In 2014, I saw an ad in The New Mexican calling for individuals willing to serve on the Santa Fe County Ethics Board. I turned in a résumé and ended up being interviewed by a couple of young women in the Santa Fe County manager's office. A week later, I was told that they had filled the position with someone else. A couple of months later, I was driving down I-40 in the Texas panhandle headed to Oklahoma when I received a call from the county manager's office asking if I would still be willing to serve on the Ethics Board. It seemed someone else had dropped out. I agreed.

For the next two years we spent most of the time revising the regulations and policies and so forth for the Ethics Board. They never had a case while I was there. When the president of the board made a presentation in 2015 to the Santa Fe County Commissioners, she was asked that, since the board had been in existence for three years, why we never had had a case. Her reply was, "Perhaps there were no ethics violations in Santa Fe County." The entire room erupted in laughter.

Senior Citizen Center Volunteer Handyman

Cliff Harris, a friend from the La Fonda dance crowd and member of my bocce ball group, talked me into joining him as a volunteer handyman for the Santa Fe Senior Citizen Center. This involved filling out some forms and providing proof of a driver's license and so forth. In that capacity, we were insured by the city.

The work was mostly for old and poor senior citizens who were trying to stay in their houses and needed certain repairs done that they could not afford. Often, there was a breakdown in communications between the person who had fretted about the problem for months before calling the coordinator at the senior citizen center and in the translation to the handyman. I would typically get an email from the coordinator at the senior citizen center describing what needed to be done and asking whether I could do it. Most often I could now include drywall.

Subsequently, Cliff traded up to Habitat for Humanity and left me as the sole handyman for the Senior Citizen Center.

One of the first jobs I had early on was a call about a lady having a problem with her heat. I drove to the lady's location near the Pacheco post office. I knocked on the door, and a little old lady answered. She weighed about eighty-five pounds, was about 85 years old, and was using a walker.

I asked what the problem was with the heat. She led me back to the hallway and pointed out that she had no thermostat. When she wanted the heat to come on, she would just twist the low voltage wires together. When it got too hot, she would untwist them. It had probably been that way ever since her husband died, and someone had knocked the old thermostat off the wall.

I went to a nearby Ace Hardware and picked up a $17 thermostat. I attached the thermostat to the wall and showed her how to use it. I then asked her if there were any other problems. There are always other problems. With tears in her eyes, she replied that her garbage disposal was broken but that she had no money for a new one. I got down on the floor under the sink and pushed the reset button on the machine. It made a sound, so I knew it was hooked up to electricity. She was on her walker looking down at me on her kitchen floor. I asked her if she had a broom anywhere, and she pointed out a broom over in the corner. I got the broom handle and wiggled it down inside the garbage disposal to free it up. I then flipped on the switch, and it ran like new. I was out of there in five minutes, and she thought I was a genius. I keep getting thank you letters from her. These folks were supposed to pay for parts, but I seldom ever charged them.

Another call involved a lady who needed a light bulb replaced and had a crack in her bathtub. The tub problem did not seem to make sense to me. Apparently, thirty or so years ago they installed lots of plastic-lined bathtubs in Santa Fe that now are beginning to have cosmetic problems. When I arrived at the location, the resident turned out to be a little Hispanic lady about four feet tall. She just could not reach the light bulb over the bathroom sink. I promptly unscrewed the old bulb and screwed in the new one. I then asked about the problem with the bathtub. She pointed out that it had a chip in it. I had some silicone caulk; I smoothed over the chip and wiped it with a cloth. Again, I was out of there in five minutes. She thanked me all the way to the door.

One lady lived in a double-wide trailer. She had a handicap ramp of four-by-eight plywood which had rotted to the point that one could step through the holes. I ended up replacing rotten boards and rebuilt her entire deck.

That turned out to be one of the biggest projects I have completed, and I had a thousand dollars of my own money in it, counting the material and paying for a couple of my helpers. She was being cited by the city for the problem, and the homeowner's group that owned the development were complaining to her. We also fixed her fence and got her car running.

For an old Hispanic man named Carlos, I replaced two doors and cleaned up his overgrown lot, hauling off two truckloads of debris. He called me his angel.

These are just a few of the dozens of calls over the past several years. These included, but were not limited to, lighting pilot lights, patching leaky roofs, unstopping sinks, fixing leaky faucets, replacing light switches, replacing light fixtures, repairing fences, and installing grab bars and handicap ramps. I jokingly say, "Install a grab bar and they fall for you." But then many of my clients are in their nineties and on walkers.

In 2018, I was selected as one of the ten volunteers that year who made a difference in an annual recognition by the Santa Fe New Mexican newspaper. The editor followed me around a couple of days with a photographer and wrote a nice puff piece... My five minutes of fame.

Conclusion

If you have read this far, you have noticed that I have been lucky enough to have had lots of different life experiences—and still lived to talk about them. They say, "luck trumps smarts every time," and I have been incredibly lucky with having so many great opportunities. Some takeaways from a life well lived include the observation that the secret to health and success comes from picking the right parents and not smoking. At least these worked for me over the years, now at the age 86 as I write.

I am reminiscent of the old saw, "Be nice to people on your way up as you may meet them on your way down." My old police Lieutenant implored us young officers to "shake a hand when you can, make a friend when you can," and "not to police one's neighbors." One of my favorites is the observation attributed to General Omar Bradley: "Good judgment comes from experience and experience comes from bad judgment." Boy, have I had lots of experience! To live through it all again, I would make most of the same mistakes I made the first time around, and I learned from each one of them.

My grandmother George opined that "he is best educated who has touched life in most places." People are not going to come knock on your door and ask you to come play with them. One must get out and off the sofa to meet and network with people who can help you and make your life better.

I am so grateful that I was able to break into the workforce as a young kid. Kids now do not have the opportunities that I enjoyed.

I have made it a point, when at all possible, to arrive on time and preferably to be early. By doing so, one has time to adjust to the problems that may arise at the last minute. That might be the traffic jam enroute or the flight that has just been canceled. One can be first in line to take one the few vacancies on the next available flight to your destination. You get to the cocktail party early so that you can greet arrivals instead of trying to break into a group already engaged in conversation. It is inconsiderate to the host if they must adjust to a guest's tardiness.

I usually have a road map to where I want to end up as well as an escape plan if needed. These do not necessarily need to be in writing, but one needs to keep them in mind. I have always tried to leave the job better than I found it to make it easier for my replacement. I have learned to seize every opportunity for training or self-improvement to remain competitive and to keep a to-do list to check off completions.

I am especially grateful to have made it this far and do believe my life has been well lived. Milking all those cows was such a great motivator to do other interesting things.

Appendix

Peyton, Jan, Tom, and Lee

Peyton's great great grandfather, Russel George
Alabama Company F

Peyton and his prize Holstein

SCOUT CAR DIVISION

OFFICER _W. George_   July 19__

DATE	1	2	3	4	5	6	7	8	9	10	11	12	13	14	15	16	17	18	19	20	21	22	23	24	25	26	27	28	29	30	31	TOTAL
CALLS	2	3	4	4	2	6	5	8	8	5	10	8	9	2	9	4	4		4	4		5	3	5								
MOV. VIOL.	5	9	9	7	11	5	2	4	7	1	7	8	1	4	5	8	1	2	4	2	4	11	6	13								30
PARK. TKS.					1			1		2				2	1		7			4	2											30
WARN. TKS.				1																												1
PICK-UP L.																																
ASSISTS	1				1																	3										5
ACC. INV.																																
MISC. ARR.	2	2	5		1	8	4		4	4	5					4	2	3	2	2	1	2	1									54
BURGLARS																																
ROBBERS																																
FELONS																																
STOLEN CAR	1			1													1															3
JUV. CO.																					1											1
JUV. HOME	5		1																													6
JUV. Y.B.																																
HDS. SPEC.																																
HDS. COURT												2																				2
FIRE CALLS																																
MENTAL P.																																
INV.													2	1																		3
ALIAS W.	3	5					6	2				2	10					4	3		2											45

Peyton's FBI training in Hogan's Alley

Clive Rigdon's vehicles

Viktor Kopytin, KGB agent (left)

ИНТЕРКОН, МОСКВА

Олег Данилович Калугин
Председатель

20005 г. Вашингтон, Округ Колумбия
Северо-Запад, ул. 15, д. 725, сунт 908
Тел: (202) 347-2624 Факс (202) 347-4631
Россия, 101000, Москва, ул. Мясницкая д. 2/15
Тел: (095) 928-1227 Факс (095) 975-2629

Tel: (202) 347-2624 Fax: (202) 347-4631
2/15 Mansnyka Street, Moscow, 101000, Russia
Tel: (095) 928-1227 Fax: (095) 975-

Director of the Administrative
Division when he retired in 1976

In 1979 he moved to Myrtle
Beach where he was an avid golfer
and a member of Pine Lakes Inter-
national Country Club and The
Dunes Golf and Beach Club. He
was a member of St. Andrew
Church, past chairman of the
Carolina Grand Strand Chapter of
the Society. He also served as co-
chairman of the Horry County
Republican party from 1991 to
1993, and was named Republican
Party volunteer of the year in 1992.
From 1993 until his death he was a
member of the Horry County
Election Commission.

Survivors include his wife,
Mildred Allen Walsh; a son,
Eugene F. Walsh of VA (a current
Special Agent of the FBI); three

daughters, Carolyn Hasfurte
Gaithersburg MD, Irene Lor
of Grayslake IL, and Constar
McFadden of Ashburn VA; a
twin sister, Dr. Jane DiPaola
Cheyenne WY and Greenacr
City FL; eight grandchildren
one great grandchild.

Ralph H. Winton

Ralph H. Winton
(1934-45) died
from a heart
attack on
October 20,
1997 at San
Antonio TX. He
was 90.

growuate in Baylor University and
St. Mary's University Law School.
After his Bureau service he was
the San Antonio City Manager and
later a San Antonio City Councilman. He was past president of the
San Antonio Livestock Exposition
and a former Director of the
National Conference of Christians
and Jews.

He is survived by his wife of
38 years, Ada; two grandchildren
and four great-grandchildren.

Former KGB Chief of Counterintelligence and Major General Oleg Kalugin under escort by Former SAs Feuer and George - Former SAs Robert W. Feuer (left) (1950-79) and W. Peyton George (1962-89) (right) were joined for lunch at the City Club in Washington, DC on November 18, 1997 by a former adversary, retired KGB Major General Oleg Kalugin. General Kalugin was the deputy KGB Resident at the Soviet Embassy in the late 1960's while both Feuer and George served on KGB squads at WFO. He went on to become Chief of the First Directorate and a Major General of the KGB. General Kalugin now heads Intercon International, USA, a consulting firm for US companies that conduct business in Russia and the newly independent states. General Kalugin autographed his book "In Bob Feuer with warm memories of the old days from a friend who was mistaken for a foe."

Peyton and friends (Oleg Kalugin and Robert W. Feuer)

Captain of the SS Manhattan tanker, Peyton,
Secretary of Agriculture Earl Butz, and Senator John Tower

Peyton and Secretary of Agriculture Earl Butz

Concealed carry group at the ABQ Police Range

General Richard H. Thompson,
Peyton's company commander for basic training at Fort Chaffee

Peyton at Fort Bragg

Peyton, Nancy, and Reba McEntire

Peyton and former President Donald Trump

To Peyton George
With best wishes,

Peyton and Henry Kissinger

To Peyton George, With Best Wishes, Gerald Ford

Peyton and former President Gerald Ford

Peyton, Nancy, Laura Bush, and former President Bush

Made in the USA
Coppell, TX
14 January 2025

44398146R00134